MARY MEADE

Chicago Tribune

"My Mind is in the Dishes"

Terence

TALKING ABOUT CAKES

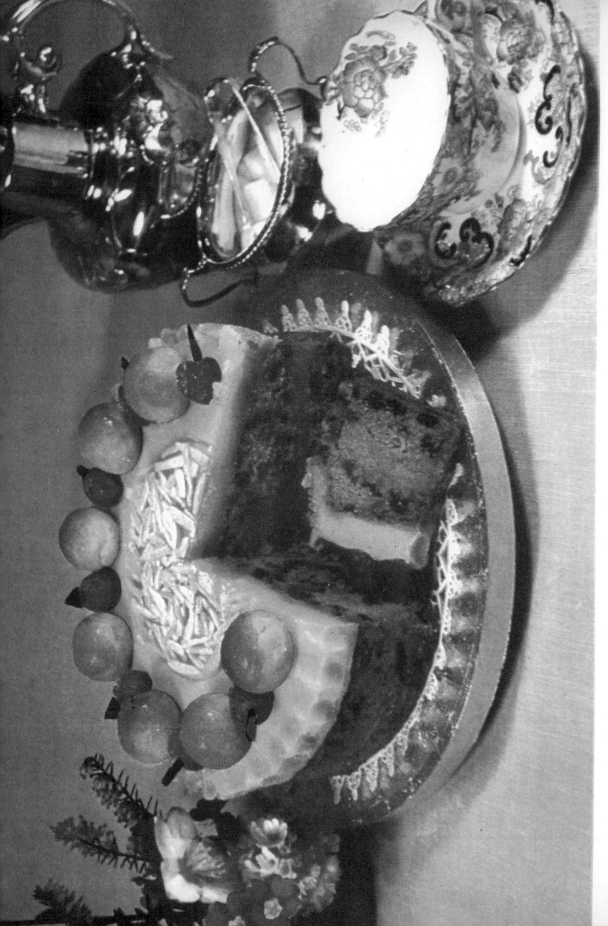

Frontispiece : Simnel Cake

TALKING
ABOUT CAKES

with an Irish and Scottish Accent

BY

MARGARET BATES

PHOTOGRAPHS BY

WILLIAM LITTLE, A. R. P. S.

JOAN LITTLE

and the author

A Pergamon Press Book

THE MACMILLAN COMPANY

NEW YORK

1964

THE MACMILLAN COMPANY
60 Fifth Avenue
New York 11, N.Y.

This book is distributed by
THE MACMILLAN COMPANY
pursuant to a special arrangement with
PERGAMON PRESS LIMITED
Oxford, England

MADE IN GREAT BRITAIN

This book is dedicated
with love and gratitude
TO MY FAMILY
who make all things possible

ACKNOWLEDGEMENT

MY sincere thanks are due to Miss Joyce Stewart, Principal of the City of Belfast College of Domestic Science for her valuable advice, and for allowing the facilities of the college at the time the photographs were taken

HOME-MADE

THE adjective "home-made" is one which rings of the highest praise when used in connection with cakes. Perhaps when applied to other things it may have a disparaging sound, but here it conjures up many lovely pictures in our minds—the wonderful aroma in the kitchen while the baking is in progress, the tea-table laden with good things—from the oven-fresh scones to the finger of plum cake, and finally the glamour of icing, and the iced cake.

In this book I wish to talk about the home-made cakes which have given me pleasure both to make and to eat, and to share the ideas and recipes which have fallen my way. I hope readers will also find enjoyment and profit in the collection which follows.

CONTENTS

Contents

Contents

xi

Contents

xii

LIST OF ILLUSTRATIONS

List of illustrations

List of illustrations

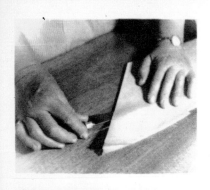

FIG. 1 (I–V) *Making and Using a Paper Icing Bag* for use with rimless icing tubes

(I) Start with a double strip of greaseproof paper, the width being equal to one-third the width of a full sheet of greaseproof paper. Fold, so as to give a right-angled triangle. One of the points should be slightly blunted as seen in the illustration

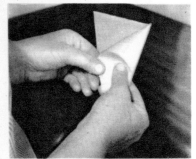

(II) Hold the triangle of paper in the right hand catching it by the apex, and having the blunt point to the right. Then using the left hand, curl the blunt point over to start forming the bag

(III) Now hold the bag with the left hand while the right hand curls the remaining point into place to form a bag with a sharp point. Finally, fold the ends twice to the inside of the bag, to hold all in position

(IV) Cut off the point of the bag and drop the icing tube inside. Then, using a teaspoon, fill the bag with icing. Only a small quantity should be used. Finally, fold the edges of the opening neatly over the icing

(V) To pipe—hold the bag between the first and second fingers of the right hand, and press with the thumb. The fingers of the left hand are only required to guide and steady the work

SOME IRISH SPECIALITIES

IN Ireland we are justly proud of our home-made breads, both oven and griddle varieties. Just to name them whets the family appetite—soda bread, wheaten farls, treacle bread, potato cake, boxty and the rest. All these items are dearly beloved. They call for deftness in the mixing and generosity in the serving, being at their best while fresh and thickly spread with butter, perhaps accompanied by the best jams and jellies of the house.

These are all traditional items and the recipes and methods have been handed down through the years. Long ago, and still in the remote parts of the country, these breads and cakes were cooked over an open turf fire in either a pot oven or on a heavy, black iron griddle. Many of us look back on such methods with nostalgia as we claim that no bread ever tasted so good. So it did taste good, but times have changed, and in some respects the making of these breads has changed too, to the housewife's advantage I may add.

MODERN FLOURS

Nowadays there is a considerable range of flours on the market and, for good results, it is wise to select flour according to the purpose for which it is used. The difference in flours is largely a difference in gluten content. This may also be described as a difference in the strength of the flour and for making soda bread and other such items a medium strength one is desirable. Few breads demonstrate the quality of a flour so clearly as soda bread and for those interested, there is on the market a special product called "Soda Bread Self-raising Flour." This can be depended upon to give excellent results. All that is required is the addition of salt and enough buttermilk to give a soft dough.

Buttermilk is not always available but sour milk may be used in its place. Alternatively a special soda-bread mix may be purchased, which only requires the addition of water. This gives excellent results, and is greatly appreciated by Irish folk living abroad.

BAKING GRIDDLE BREAD

Nowadays few of us use the traditional iron griddle, for it is not very efficient on our modern cookers. To use it successfully one requires gentle, even heat such as was possible from a well-made bed of turf coals. However, those who have a gas cooker may purchase a special gas griddle which is excellent to use; owners of electric cookers will find that the gently heated grill or hot-plate is also splendid; while those who rejoice in an electric frying-pan will find this unsurpassed for making griddle breads. It is blessed with a lid which helps the baking process considerably, the retained steam keeping the farls wonderfully soft, while there is thermostatic heat control in the handle which makes exact work easy.

Whatever the griddle it should be heated gently to get good results. If bread is to be baked on the electric grill or hot-plate the heat should be switched to "low" both while it is heating up and in use. To test the heat sprinkle a little flour over the cooking surface; when correctly heated it should tint the flour in a minute or so. A griddle required for dropped scones or potato cake should be tested for heat at the same time as it is being greased. Rub with a piece of fat, preferably a lump of suet or butter. In melting, the fat should smoke slightly if the griddle is hot enough for either of these items.

IRISH SODA BREAD

1 lb flour	*½ teaspoon cream of tartar*
1 teaspoon salt	*buttermilk or sour milk to mix*
½ teaspoon baking soda	

Alternatively, use "Soda Bread—Self-raising flour" and only add salt and buttermilk or sour milk to mix.

Sieve the flour, salt, baking soda and cream of tartar into a bowl. Be careful to avoid all lumps in the soda, and if necessary crush in the palm of the hand before sieving. Then, using a metal spoon, mix lightly and quickly with the buttermilk; add just sufficient to give a soft, but not sticky, dough. It is difficult to give an exact quantity of milk as this varies with the flour.

Turn the dough on to a lightly-floured board and shape into a round cake using floured hands. Cut into four farls and either bake in a hot oven or cook on the griddle.

Suggested oven temperatures are 7, F or 450°, and the cake of bread will require approximately 30 minutes, according to the thickness of the farls.

If cooked on the griddle, turn after 5–7 minutes, when it should be nicely browned on the underside and complete the cooking on the other side.

Soda bread is all the softer for being wrapped in the folds of a clean cloth, to cool.

A COARSE WHEATEN BREAD

12 oz wheaten meal	*1 teaspoon salt*
2 oz bran	*1½ oz margarine (optional)*
2–4 oz flour	*approx ¾–1 pint buttermilk or*
1 small teaspoon baking soda	*sour milk to mix*

Put the meal, bran and flour into a mixing bowl. Then crush the lumps from the soda and add, together with the salt. If there is margarine available, rub in a little, as it will make the bread keep better. Next mix all to a soft dough with buttermilk. Turn on to a board sprinkled with wheaten meal and form into a round cake. Mark into four farls and bake in a hot oven, either on a floured baking sheet or in an 8-inch tin. The bread will take approximately 30 minutes or more, according to the thickness of the farls, and suggested oven temperatures are 7, F or 450°.

A FINE-TEXTURED BROWN BREAD

For those who do not care for a very coarse bread the following recipe is more suitable.

¾ lb wholemeal	*1 teaspoon cream of tartar*
¼ lb flour	*1 teaspoon syrup*
1 teaspoon salt	*buttermilk or sour milk to mix*
1 small teaspoon baking soda	

Crush the lumps from the soda and sieve with the flour, salt and cream of tartar. Add the wholemeal. Rub in the syrup and 1½ oz margarine if wished. Next mix all to a soft dough with buttermilk. Turn on to a board sprinkled with wholemeal and pat into a round flat cake. Cut into 4 farls and bake in a hot oven either on a floured baking sheet or in an 8-inch tin. The bread will take approximately 30 minutes, according to the thickness of the farls, and suggested oven temperatures are 7, F or 450°.

Cool, wrapped in a clean cloth.

BAKED IN A SAUCEPAN

A favourite method for baking bread is to cook it in a strong saucepan with the lid on. In this way the steam is retained and the bread is pleasantly moist to eat.

Use any of the above three recipes in this way. Prepare a 7-inch saucepan by lining the bottom with a circle of margarine paper and greasing the bottom and sides of the pan well. Turn the dough into the saucepan and neaten with a fork. The cake is more attractive if the surface is left rough. Put the lid on the pan and place all in a hot oven. As the bread is fairly thick it will require approximately 30–40 minutes to bake. Suggested oven temperatures are 7, F or 450°. The bread generally browns even with the lid on, but if not, remove it for the last 10 minutes.

TREACLE BREAD

1 lb flour	*2 oz margarine*
1 teaspoon salt	*2 tablespoons sugar*
1 teaspoon baking soda	*2 tablespoons treacle*
1 teaspoon cream of tartar	*sweet milk to mix*

Sieve the flour, salt, soda and cream of tartar together. Cut and rub in the margarine and add the sugar. Put the treacle in a bowl and thin down with some milk. Use this, together with more milk as necessary, to mix the dry ingredients to a fairly stiff dough. Turn on to a floured board. Using floured hands, pat into a flat round cake. Cut into four farls and lift on to a floured baking sheet. Bake in a hot oven for approximately 30 minutes, according to the thickness of the bread, suggested oven temperatures being 7, F or 450°.

Cool, wrapped in a clean cloth.

Alternatively bake the treacle bread on the griddle.

4

RICH SLIM CAKES

½ lb flour	2 oz castor sugar
½ teaspoon salt	2 oz sultanas
¼ teaspoon baking soda	a little buttermilk to mix
4 oz margarine	

Sieve the flour, salt and baking soda, making sure there are no lumps in the soda. Cut and rub in the margarine, then add the sugar and sultanas. Mix all to a stiff dough with buttermilk. Turn on to a floured board and roll out a quarter of an inch thick. Cut into rounds and bake on a moderately-heated griddle, turning when nicely browned on the under side.

Serve very fresh with butter.

POTATO CAKE

No exact recipe is necessary for making potato cake and the following quantities are intended only as a guide for those making it for the first time.

1 lb cooked potatoes	1–2 oz margarine
1 teaspoon salt	approx 4 tablespoons flour

Potato cake is better if made from freshly-cooked, hot potatoes, but cold ones left over from a meal often suffice.

Put the cooked potatoes through a potato ricer. Add the salt. If hot, it is sufficient to add the margarine as it is, for it will soon melt. Otherwise it is necessary to melt it in a saucepan before adding. Now work in the flour, the amount varying slightly with the type of potato, but sufficient to bind the whole into a dough. Cut the mixture in two and roll each piece into a circular shape about a ¼-inch thick. Cut into 6 or 8 farls and bake on a hot, greased griddle. Turn once, when well browned on the under side.

SWEET POTATO CAKE

A fresh autumn evening, with a nip in the air, is the time to make this delicious variation of potato cake.

5

Make the potato cake as in the previous recipe, only roll it into a thick round. It should be fully ½-inch thick, and it is cut into squares (that is, as far as one can cut a circle into squares). Cook these on a well-greased griddle and when well-browned on both sides, split and fill with a slice cut from a block of butter. Sprinkle generously with sugar and close. Pile in a deep dish such as a soup plate and keep hot until all are cooked. A most lovely "gravy" runs from the potato cake, and the whole makes wonderful eating.

A more sophisticated version of this country dish is as follows:—the potato cake is rolled out very thinly and cut into rounds with a 4–5-inch cutter. Cook on a hot, greased griddle and when well browned on both sides, spread with butter, sprinkle with sugar and roll up like pancakes. Serve very hot.

POTATO APPLE CAKE
a delicacy from the orchard districts of Co. Armagh

For this version of an apple cake, potato cake is used instead of the more conventional pastry. To the uninitiated this may not sound good to eat, but in fact the flavour of the potatoes combines very well with the apples. Traditionally this form of apple cake is baked on the griddle, and the apples are not generally sweetened until the cake is cooked, otherwise the syrup oozes out and burns. When cooked, the potato cake making the covering is folded back and the apples underneath well sprinkled with sugar. This should be followed by a good slice of butter and the lid replaced. The heat of the cake will soon melt it into a glorious juice.

No exact recipe is really necessary. Begin by making potato cake as already described. Then cut the dough in two and roll each piece into a circular shape. Peel and chop a few apples until very fine. Spread over one piece of potato cake and cover with the second piece. Neaten the edges by pinching round as for a piece of shortbread. Bake gently on both sides on a greased griddle. When well browned, open, sprinkle with sugar and add a generous slice of butter. Close again and serve very hot.

BOXTY PANCAKES

Boxty pancakes are robust fare associated with the potato harvest in such parts of Ireland as counties Tyrone, Leitrim and Cavan. The story is that when workers collected on a farm to help with the lifting of the potatoes, the large potatoes, too big for storing,

PLATE 1. *A still life from an Irish kitchen,* showing a round of wheaten bread, soda farls, scones, boxty pancakes and sweet potato cake as well as an old iron griddle and harnen stand alongside the modern frying pan. The latter makes an excellent "griddle" for baking bread

were grated and made into boxty pancakes. Incredible as it seems to me, a mere town dweller, a bucketful of these potatoes were prepared for boxty for the evening meal of the farm hands. The grater used was home-made and of a size in proportion to the task to be done. The recipe which follows is an adaptation of that used on the farms, and not of such magnitude, but suitable to suburban homes. The pancakes are so good to eat that it would seem a pity if they should be forgotten.

4–5 large potatoes	½ teaspoon salt
2 tablespoons flour	milk to mix
1 teaspoon baking powder	
½–1 teaspoon caraway seeds if wished	

Peel and grate the potatoes and squeeze as dry as possible in a strong cloth. Keep the liquid and put aside for 4–5 hours, when a starchy sediment will settle out. This is required later when mixing the batter. Meanwhile keep the grated potato tightly screwed up in the cloth. Set it in a bowl and cover with a plate, so that the air cannot cause it to discolour too much. A little discoloration is bound to take place and will do no harm. This preparation is generally done in the morning and then the ingredients are ready to make into pancakes at tea-time.

Put all the dry ingredients and the grated potato into a bowl. Pour off the liquid in the other bowl and add the sediment which remains to the rest of the ingredients. Mix to a fairly soft batter with milk, the consistency being such that it is necessary to help it to spread in the frying pan. Heat a good lump of butter in a small pan. An omelet pan, if not too sacred, is ideal and when hot pour in some of the mixture, spreading with a spoon. Fry until well browned on both sides and serve hot either with fried bacon or with plenty of butter and sugar.

Sometimes a few caraway seeds are added to the batter if their flavour is appreciated in the household.

GOOD SCONE RECIPES

A GOOD scone should be as soft as sponge and deftness is required in the making. Remember, they should be quickly and lightly mixed and baked in a hot oven. Serve while fresh, with plenty of butter.

SULTANA SCONES

½ lb flour
1 teaspoon baking powder
½ teaspoon salt
2 oz margarine

1 oz sugar
2 oz sultanas
1 oz candied lemon peel
milk to mix

Sieve the flour, baking powder and salt and cut and rub in the margarine. Add the sugar, sultanas and peel and mix to a soft, but not sticky dough, using the milk. Turn on to a floured board, toss over and pat out about 1-inch thick. Cut into scones, brush with egg or milk and bake in a hot oven for 15 minutes (8, G or 475°).

VERY LIGHT SCONES

There is a surprisingly large proportion of baking powder in this recipe for sultana scones. They are therefore, very light, particularly while rising in the oven. On this account they should not be moved until they are baked.

½ lb flour
1 dessertspoon baking powder
½ teaspoon salt
2 oz margarine

1 oz castor sugar
1 oz sultanas
½ oz candied lemon peel
milk to mix

Sieve the flour, baking powder and salt, and cut and rub in the margarine. Add the sugar, sultanas and peel, and mix all to a soft dough with milk. Turn on to a floured board, pat out about 1-inch thick and cut into scones. Brush with egg or milk and bake in a hot oven for 15 minutes (8, G or 475°).

COCONUT SCONES

½ lb flour	2½ oz castor sugar
1 teaspoon baking powder	1½ oz coconut
½ teaspoon salt	vanilla essence
4 oz margarine	1 egg and a little milk to mix

Sieve the flour, baking powder and salt and cut and rub in the margarine. Keep aside a dessertspoonful each of the sugar and coconut and add the remainder to the flour. Mix all to a soft dough using the vanilla essence, beaten egg and a little milk. Turn on to a floured board, roll or pat out and cut into scones. Brush with egg or milk and dip in the left-over sugar and coconut. Bake in a hot oven for 15 minutes (8, G or 475°).

DATE SCONES

½ lb flour	1 oz sugar
2 teaspoons baking powder	2 oz chopped dates
½ teaspoon salt	1 teaspoon treacle
¼ teaspoon ground cinnamon	milk to mix
1 oz margarine	

Sieve all the dry ingredients and cut and rub in the margarine. Add the sugar and the chopped dates. Combine the treacle with some of the milk and use to mix all to a soft dough. Roll out and cut into scones. Brush with egg or milk and bake in a hot oven for 15 minutes (8, G or 475°).

FRENCH SCONES

10 oz flour	3 oz castor sugar
½ teaspoon baking soda	1 egg

1 teaspoon cream of tartar
1/2 teaspoon salt
3 oz margarine

2–3 tablespoons raspberry jam
milk to mix

Sieve the flour, baking soda, cream of tartar and salt. Cut and rub in the margarine and add the sugar. Mix all to a soft dough with the beaten egg and milk. Toss on to a floured board and cut in two. Roll one half to fit a swiss-roll tin. Spread with raspberry jam. Cover with the second piece of scone dough and bake in a hot oven for 20–30 minutes (7, F or 450°). Cut into fingers and dredge generously with icing sugar.

GINGER AND WALNUT SCONES

1/2 lb flour
1 teaspoon baking powder
1/2 teaspoon salt
2 oz margarine
1 oz castor sugar

2 oz chopped preserved ginger
1 oz chopped walnuts
1 egg
milk to mix

Sieve the dry ingredients, and cut and rub in the margarine. Add the sugar, chopped preserved ginger and chopped walnuts. Beat the egg and add a little milk. Use to mix all to a soft dough. Turn on to a floured board, toss over and roll out about 1-inch thick. Cut into scones, brush with egg and bake in a hot oven for 15 minutes (8, G or 475°).

LITTLE TEA CAKES
my own favourite

1/2 lb flour
1 teaspoon baking powder
1/2 teaspoon salt
4 oz margarine
2 1/2 oz castor sugar

1 1/2 oz sultanas
1 dessertspoon chopped peel
1 egg
milk to mix

Sieve the first three ingredients together and cut and rub in the margarine. Add the sugar, sultanas and peel and mix all to a soft dough, using the beaten egg and milk.

Turn on to a floured board, roll out and cut into scones. Brush with egg and bake in a hot oven for 15 minutes (8, G or 475°).

MILK ROLLS

½ lb flour	½ teaspoon salt
¼ teaspoon baking soda	2 oz margarine
½ teaspoon cream of tartar	sweet milk to mix

Sieve the flour, baking soda, cream of tartar and salt together. Rub in the margarine and mix all to a soft dough with sweet milk. Roll out about ¼-inch thick and cut into squares. Fold in two and bake in a hot oven for 15 minutes (8, G or 475°).

MONTREAL SCONES

½ lb flour	4 oz sultanas
2 teaspoons baking powder	1 oz flaked almonds
1 teaspoon salt	1 egg
3 oz margarine	milk to mix
1 oz sugar	

Sieve the flour with the baking powder and salt. Cut and rub in the margarine. Add the sugar, sultanas and half the almonds. Beat the egg, adding a little milk and use to mix all to a soft dough. Toss on to a floured board, roll out and cut into scones. Brush with egg and sprinkle the top with the remaining flaked almonds. Bake in a hot oven for 15 minutes.

TREACLE SCONES

½ lb flour	½ teaspoon mixed spice
½ teaspoon baking soda	1 oz margarine
1 teaspoon cream of tartar	1 oz castor sugar
½ teaspoon salt	1 tablespoon treacle
½ teaspoon ground cinnamon	milk to mix

Sieve the dry ingredients and cut and rub in the margarine. Add the sugar. Dilute the treacle with a little milk and, adding more milk as necessary, mix all to a light dough. Turn on to a floured board, toss over, roll out and cut into scones. Place on a greased or floured tray, brush with egg or milk and bake in a hot oven for 15 minutes (8, G or 475°).

GRIDDLE PANCAKES

A simple little recipe giving soft spongy pancakes which are delicious served hot with butter and honey or jam.

4 oz flour	*2 small teaspoons syrup*
1 pinch of salt	*buttermilk to mix*
½ teaspoon baking soda	

Sieve the flour, salt and baking soda into a bowl. Dilute the golden syrup with a little buttermilk and use, adding more buttermilk as necessary, to give a creamy batter. Beat with a wooden spoon until glossy and smooth. Lightly grease a hot griddle and drop the mixture on to it using a dessertspoon. When brown on one side, turn and brown on the other.

DOUGHNUTS
with baking powder

6 oz flour	*1 oz sugar*
½ teaspoon salt	*1 egg*
1 teaspoon baking powder	*milk to mix*
2 oz margarine	*a little raspberry jam*

Sieve the flour, salt and baking powder; cut and rub in the margarine. Add the sugar and mix to a light dough with the beaten egg and milk. Turn out on to a floured board and roll out ¼-inch thick. Cut into small rounds. Put a little raspberry jam on half these circles. Brush the other half with milk and put two together, pinching carefully round the edge to fasten securely. Fry in a faintly smoking pan of deep fat for 6–8 minutes, turning when brown on the underside. Toss in sugar or a mixture of sugar and ground cinnamon.

RAISED WITH YEAST

A YEAST mixture has a flavour and texture all its own and this, combined with the fascination of working with the dough and seeing it rise, makes it interesting to every housewife. The satisfaction obtained through handling the dough can be likened to the satisfaction of the potter with a lump of clay, and this basic truth explains why, in spite of excellent bread and buns being available in the shops, housewives still enjoy making their own—at least occasionally.

Where there are children in the house, yeast buns are particularly satisfactory, for they are neither too rich nor too plain for them. Indeed we adults may well envy the healthy appetites of the young as they enjoy such items as doughnuts, chelsea buns and the like. Happily for them, the middle-aged spread is not yet a problem.

A MATTER OF TEMPERATURE

When handling yeast remember that heat will kill it but that cold will only retard its growth. Usually recipe books only emphasise the need for warmth and the avoidance of draughts when making such mixtures, but it is sometimes useful to know that the process can be retarded by keeping the mixture in a cool place, even the refrigerator if necessary. A dough can be mixed and after kneading or beating, as the case may be, refrigerated. It does not need to have risen before being put away, but remember it is necessary to cover it with aluminium foil and perhaps a damp cloth to prevent a skin forming. The dough may be held in the refrigerator several hours, or until the next day, if necessary. This is obviously convenient. You will find that even in the refrigerator the rising process will take place slowly so that on removal one can usually carry on knocking it back and shaping as required. The richer the yeast mixture the longer it can be retarded in the refrigerator.

THE STORAGE OF YEAST

The correct storage of yeast often presents a problem to housewives. Usually it may be purchased from the baker, either by the ounce or the half-pound, but if you bake at all frequently it is best to buy it in fairly large amounts. It stores beautifully in the refrigerator if kept air-tight in a glass jar. Like this it will keep well for many days, even a week, and as the spirit moves you to bake it is readily available. Dried yeast may also be purchased, but for some reason most cooks prefer to use it in its natural form.

BREAD

3 lb flour	*1 oz yeast*
3 teaspoons salt	*approx 1½ pints warm water*
1 teaspoon sugar	

Add the salt and sugar to the flour and warm in a mixing bowl. Blend the yeast with the greater part of the warm water. Use to mix the flour to an elastic dough. Turn on to a floured board and knead thoroughly. Return the dough to the bowl. Cover with a damp cloth, and put to rise in a warm place. This will take approximately 1 hour or until double its original size. Turn out on to a floured board, knead lightly and cut into 3 even-sized pieces. Knead and shape each piece once more and drop into a 2 lb loaf tin. Put in a warm place for another 10–15 minutes or until the yeast begins to work again. Then bake in a hot oven for approximately 40 minutes, suggested oven temperatures being 7, F or 450°.

On removal from the oven the loaves are sometimes rubbed with a buttery paper to give a slight glaze and soften the crust.

BROWN BREAD

2 lb wholemeal	*1 teaspoon sugar*
½ lb flour	*1 oz yeast*
2½ teaspoons salt	*approx 1½–2 pints warm water*

Put the wholemeal, flour, salt and sugar into a mixing bowl and put to warm. Blend the yeast with the greater part of the warm water. Use to mix the dry ingredients to an elastic dough. Knead well on a floured board. Return the dough to the bowl and cover with a damp cloth. Put to rise until double its original size. Turn out on to a floured board, knead again and cut in two. Knead and shape each piece and drop into a 2-lb loaf tin. Prove for a further 15 minutes. Then bake in a hot oven for 50–60 minutes. Suggested oven temperatures being 7, F or 450°.

If wished, brush with butter when baked.

BRIDGE ROLLS FOR PARTY SAVOURIES

1 lb flour	approx ½ pint milk
1 teaspoon salt	2 eggs
2 teaspoons sugar	1 oz yeast
1 oz margarine	

Put the flour, salt and sugar into a bowl. Warm the milk and margarine together and add to the beaten eggs. Blend the yeast with part of the milk and eggs. Use this to mix the flour to a soft, kindly dough, adding more milk and egg as necessary. Beat thoroughly using the dough hook of the mixing machine, a wooden spoon or the hand. Leave the dough tidy in the bowl, cover with a damp cloth and put in a warm place to rise. This will take from ½–1 hour according to conditions. Now turn the mixture on to a floured board. Knead once more, roll out to about ½-inch thick and cut into bridge rolls with a suitable cutter. Arrange on a greased tray so that the rolls are just touching. Put in a warm place for another 10 minutes or until the yeast begins to work again. Brush with egg and bake in a hot oven for 12–15 minutes, suggested oven temperatures being 9, G or 475°.

If wished, poppy seed may be used scattered over the rolls after they are brushed with egg.

TEA CAKES

¾ lb flour	2 oz margarine
¾ teaspoon salt	½ pint warm milk
1 teaspoon sugar	1 egg
¾ oz yeast	

Put the flour, salt and sugar into a warm bowl. Blend the yeast with the warm milk. Melt the margarine in a small saucepan and add to the milk.

Use this, together with the beaten egg, to mix the flour to a soft dough. Beat well using the dough hook of the mixing machine, a wooden spoon or the hand. Now cover the bowl with a damp cloth and put aside in a warm place to rise until double its original size. This will take approximately ¾–1 hour. Then turn out on to a floured board. Cut into 3 portions and knead each piece until smooth. Form into round cakes and place on a greased tray. Set the cakes to rise again in a warm place for 10 minutes. Then bake in a hot oven (7, F or 450°) for approximately 15–20 minutes. When cooked brush with a heavy syrup of sugar and water or rub with buttered paper.

If wished 2 oz currants and a little candied peel may be added to this dough and the tea cakes brushed with egg and sprinkled with coarse sugar before baking.

Tea cakes should be served hot, split and heavily buttered.

CREAM COOKIES

¾ lb flour
¾ teaspoon salt
1½ oz sugar
1½ oz margarine

¾ oz yeast
approx ½–¾ pint warm water
to mix

to finish :—raspberry jam and whipped cream

Put the flour, and sugar into a bowl and rub in the margarine. Blend the yeast with the greater part of the warm water. Use to mix the flour to a soft dough, using the remaining water as necessary. Beat well using the dough hook of the mixing machine, a wooden spoon or the hand. Then cover the bowl with a damp cloth and put in a warm place to rise. This will take ½–1 hour according to conditions. Turn the dough on to a floured board, knead a little and divide into small pieces of about ¾–1 oz each. Shape each into a round bun and place on a greased tray. Put in a warm place for another 10 minutes or until the yeast begins to work again. Then bake in a hot oven (9, G or 475°) for 12–15 minutes.

When cold make a diagonal cut with a pair of scissors. Spread the opening with raspberry jam and fill with whipped cream. Serve thickly dusted with icing sugar.

ICED COOKIES

Yeast cookies, made as described in the previous recipe, may be finished with a spreading of water icing on top instead of filling them with jam and cream. Sometimes, too, the freshly iced bun is dipped into coconut for a little additional variety.

DOUGHNUTS

¾ lb flour	1½ oz margarine
¾ teaspoon salt	¾ oz yeast
1½ oz sugar	½–¾ pint warm water

to finish :—raspberry jam and sugar for tossing

Put the flour, salt and sugar into a bowl and rub in the margarine. Blend the yeast with the greater part of the warm water. Use to mix the flour to a soft dough, adding more water as necessary. Beat well using the dough hook of the mixing machine, a wooden spoon or the hand. Cover the bowl with a damp cloth and put in a warm place to rise. This will take from ½–1 hour according to conditions. When the mixture is double in size turn on to a floured board and knead lightly. Then divide into small portions of approximately ¾–1 oz each. Shape into round buns and place on a floured tray to rise for a further 10 minutes. Fry in deep fat, heated to just under the haze point, turning in the fat as necessary. Doughnuts must be cooked gently and will require from 10–15 minutes according to size. Then drain, make a diagonal cut with scissors and spread the opening with raspberry jam. Toss in sugar and serve hot. Sometimes the sugar is flavoured with ground cinnamon.

CHELSEA BUNS

1 lb flour	approx 1 gill warm milk
1 teaspoon salt	2 eggs
4 oz margarine	4 oz currants
4 oz castor sugar	¾ teaspoon mixed spice
1 oz yeast	

Raised with yeast

Put the flour and salt into a bowl and rub in half the margarine. Add 2 oz sugar. Add the warm milk to the yeast and blend. Use, together with the beaten eggs, to mix the flour to a soft dough. Beat well, then cover with a damp cloth and put to rise until doubled in bulk; 1–1½ hours should be allowed for this process. Turn the mixture on to a floured board, and knead again. Roll to a square shape. Soften the remaining 2 oz margarine and spread over the dough, sprinkle with some of the remaining sugar. Fold the dough in two and roll into a square again. Combine the remaining sugar with the currants and spice and use to sprinkle over the dough. Roll up like a swiss roll and cut off in 1½-inch lengths. Turn each piece over on to the cut surface and arrange on a greased swiss-roll tin, placing them fairly close together so that they will touch when baked. Put to prove in a warm place until the yeast begins to work again. This will take 15–20 minutes. Bake in a hot oven (7, F or 450°) for 20–30 minutes.

When cooked these buns may be brushed with a heavy syrup of sugar and water or, alternatively, iced with water icing.

HOT CROSS BUNS
for Good Friday

1 lb flour	6 oz currants
1 teaspoon mixed spice	1 oz chopped candied peel
1 teaspoon salt	approx 1–1½ gills warm water
2 oz margarine	1 oz. yeast
2 oz castor sugar	2 eggs

Sieve the flour, spice and salt into a bowl and rub in the margarine. Add the sugar, currants and peel. Blend the yeast with the milk and use, together with the beaten eggs to mix the flour to a soft dough. Beat well using the dough hook of the electric mixer, a wooden spoon or the hand. Then cover with a damp cloth and put in a warm place to rise. This will take from 1–1½ hours.

Turn the dough on to a floured board and knead lightly. Then cut into 12 even-sized pieces and shape each into a round bun. Place on a greased tray and put in a warm place for 10–15 minutes. Brush with egg and mark each with a cross using a knife, or better still make crosses from a small piece of short crust pastry. Bake in a hot oven (7, F or 450°) for 15–20 minutes.

DANISH PASTRY

The method of making Danish pastry is on much the same lines as making puff pastry, except that a rich yeast dough is used instead of the flour-and-water dough of the puff pastry. While a little troublesome to make, the finished article makes really good eating and lends itself to a great variety of finishes.

Throughout the whole process the pastry must be kept cold and where a refrigerator is available this is an ideal place to store it between rollings. Indeed Danish pastry may be stored in this way overnight, or longer, to be worked off at leisure. In putting it in the refrigerator for any length of time keep it tightly covered with aluminium foil to prevent surface drying.

Incidentally it is worth using butter when making this type of mixture, not only on account of its flavour, but also because the pastry is easier to handle. Empire butter is the best type, being suitably tough and so able to stand up to the repeated rollings.

1 lb flour	*1½ oz yeast*
1 teaspoon salt	*1½ oz melted butter for the dough*
7 fluid oz milk	*a little grated lemon rind*
2 oz castor sugar	*14 oz limpire butter for rolling in*
2 beaten eggs	

Put the flour and salt into a bowl. Combine the milk, sugar, beaten eggs, yeast, melted butter and lemon rind and stir together until quite smooth. Then use to mix the flour to a soft elastic dough. Knead a little and put aside to relax for 10–20 minutes. This rest will make the dough easier to roll later.

Meanwhile put the 14 oz butter between two pieces of greaseproof paper and roll into a square of about ¼-inch thick. Now roll the dough to a rather larger square and fold the butter in, envelope fashion.

Roll the pastry out into a strip. Fold in three, as in making one of the flaky pastries and repeat, giving it in all four rollings. Put in the refrigerator or other cool place between rollings as is found necessary.

USING THE DANISH PASTRY

The Danish pastry is now ready for working off. There are innumerable ways of doing this, but generally a filling is used, often made with ground almonds or dried fruit and candied peel. Later when the buns are baked they are brushed with hot apricot jam which has been flavoured with rum. This gives them a good eating quality and high gloss, while they are further enhanced with a little water icing. This may be spread on, but the buns are even more appetising in appearance if it is piped. This piping is not intended to be over neat or precise, but should have a casual look. To get this effect put the water icing in a paper piping bag, no pipe being necessary. Cut a little from the point of the bag and pipe the icing in a zig-zag fashion across the bun. Do this while the bun is hot from the oven when the heat will cause the icing to run attractively.

A few interesting suggestions follow for using the Danish pastry, but first of all here is the recipe for a suitable almond filling:—

ALMOND FILLING FOR DANISH PASTRY

2 oz ground almonds   *a little beaten egg*
4 oz castor sugar   *a few drops of almond essence*

Put the ground almonds and sugar into a bowl and stir in sufficient beaten egg to give a spreading consistency. Flavour with almond essence. Use as required in the following suggestions for working off the Danish pastry.

HORSE'S TEETH
a fanciful name for most attractive pastries

Take approximately $\frac{1}{4}$ lb Danish pastry and roll into a rectangular shape and approximately $\frac{1}{4}$-inch thick. Cut by the length into 2-inch wide strips. Now spread one half of each strip lightly with the almond filling. Sprinkle well with currants and fold in two by the length. Roll again in order to press the currants well home. Cut into $2\frac{1}{2}$–3-inch pieces, and finish each by cutting 5 or 6 "teeth" along the cut edge. Place on a greased tray curving each into a crescent. Put in very gentle heat until the yeast begins to work, remembering that at this stage excessive heat will cause the butter to run out. Then bake in a moderately hot oven (6–5, E–D or 400°) for approximately 15–20 minutes. Immediately they are baked, brush with hot apricot jam flavoured with rum, and pipe with a little water icing in a zig-zag fashion. Alternatively sprinkle the apricot jam with toasted flaked almonds.

ALMOND PUFFS

Using about a ¼ lb Danish pastry roll out approximately ⅛-inch thick. Cut into 4-inch squares. Brush with egg and put a teaspoonful of the almond filling in the centre. Now take two opposite corners and press into the centre, follow with the remaining two to form a cushion. Place on a greased tray and put in gentle heat until the yeast begins to work. Then bake in a moderately hot oven (6–5, E–D or 400°) for approximately 15–20 minutes. Finish as already described brushing with hot rum and apricot jam and piping with white water icing.

DANISH ALMOND BUNS

Roll out a piece of Danish pastry into a rectangular shape and approximately ¼-inch thick. Spread lightly with the almond filling and sprinkle with currants. Roll up like a swiss roll and cut into 1–1½-inch pieces. Turn each piece over on to the cut surface and arrange fairly closely on a greased tray. Place in a gentle heat to prove, then bake in a moderate oven (6–5, E–D or 400°) for approximately 20 minutes. When cold finish the top of each pastry with water icing and sprinkle with flaked browned almonds.

DANISH ALMOND TWISTS

Roll out some Danish pastry to a rectangular shape, the length being approximately 10 inches and about ¼-inch thick. Spread half this area lightly with the almond mixture and sprinkle with currants. Fold in two by the length and roll heavily to press the fruit home. Then cut into strips about ½-inch wide. These strips are now twisted individually. This is easily done by using a pushing movement with one hand and a pulling movement with the other. One end of the strip should be tapered. Now make it into a flat coil using the narrow end for the centre and tucking the last bit underneath the outer circle to make all secure. Arrange on a greased tray and prove in gentle heat. Then bake in a moderately hot oven (6–5, E–D or 400°). While still hot brush with heated apricot jam flavoured with rum and pipe a zig-zag line of water icing across each bun.

DANISH ALMOND CRESCENTS

Roll out the Danish pastry to about $\frac{1}{4}$-inch thick and cut into strips approximately 4-inch wide and from this cut triangles having bases of $2\frac{3}{4}$-inch in length. Make a little slit in the apex of each pendant shape. Spread the base with a little almond filling and roll up, tending to pull on the point and catching the end underneath. Place on a greased tray in the form of crescents (or leave as they are). Prove in gentle heat and bake in a moderately hot oven (6–5, E–D or 400°) for 15–20 minutes. While hot from the oven brush with heated apricot jam flavoured with rum and pipe a zig-zag line of water icing along each.

LARGE ALMOND RING

Roll out a piece of Danish pastry to a piece approximately 14 inches long and 6 inches wide. Spread with the almond mixture and roll up as for a swiss roll, brushing the last $\frac{1}{2}$-inch with egg or water to make a seal. This should be kept underneath. Bring the two ends together and join neatly. Place on a greased tray and prove in gentle heat. When the yeast is beginning to work, brush the ring with egg and sprinkle with flaked almonds. Bake in a moderately hot oven (5, D or 375°) for approximately 40 minutes. Finally ice with a little water icing.

MAKE THEM RICH

ROCK buns are simple little cakes which every cook will know, but I wonder if you have found, as I have, that there is a great difference even in these. They can be either very delicious to eat or uninteresting and heavy going. The difference is largely due to the amount of fat used in the recipe and I believe it pays to make them really rich.

EASY AND CONVENIENT

Rock buns are the best known of a great family of recipes made by what is spoken of as the "rubbing-in method" whereby the fat is rubbed into the flour until it resembles crumbs. This is an easy and convenient way of combining the ingredients and is therefore very practical in day-to-day baking. I particularly like rock buns when they are made with soft brown sugar, and with plenty of chopped ginger, cherries and walnuts, instead of the more usual currants. I also use chopped dates when I have nothing else and the result is most pleasing.

RICH ROCK BUNS

It is useful to know that if ½ lb of flour is used you may expect to obtain between 16 and 18 little cakes.

½ lb flour	*1½ oz glacé cherries*
1 teaspoon baking powder	*1½ oz china ginger*
pinch of salt	*1½ oz walnuts*
4 oz margarine	*1 egg*
4 oz soft brown sugar	

Sieve the flour, baking powder and salt into a bowl. Cut and rub in the margarine. Add the brown sugar, the chopped cherries, ginger and nuts. Mix all to a very stiff dough with beaten egg. Arrange the mixture in small rough heaps on a greased baking sheet and bake in a hot oven for 15 minutes, (7, F or 450°).

DATE AND WALNUT BUNS

½ lb flour
1 teaspoon baking powder
¼ teaspoon baking soda
½ teaspoon salt
4 oz margarine

4 oz soft brown sugar
3 oz chopped dates
2 oz chopped walnuts
1 egg
a little milk if necessary

Sieve the flour with the baking powder, soda and salt. Cut and rub in the margarine and add the sugar, dates and nuts. Mix all to a very stiff consistency with the beaten egg, adding a little milk if necessary. Arrange the mixture in small rough heaps on a greased baking sheet and bake in a hot oven for 15 minutes, (7, F or 450°).

DATE SHORTCAKE

½ lb flour
1 teaspoon baking powder
6 oz margarine

4 oz soft brown sugar
6 oz chopped dates

Cut and rub the margarine into the flour and baking powder. Add the sugar and the chopped dates and mix well together. Press into a shallow rectangular tin. The mixture should be approximately ½-inch thick. Bake in a moderate oven for 30–40 minutes. Cut into fingers and serve dusted with castor sugar.

APPLE FINGERS
good when served fresh from the oven and still warm

10 oz flour
1¼ teaspoons baking powder
a pinch of salt
5 oz margarine

5 oz soft brown sugar
3 cooking apples
1 egg
a little milk

Sieve the flour, baking powder and salt together, and cut and rub in the margarine. Add the sugar and the chopped apples and mix to a dry dough with the beaten egg and milk. Press into a greased swiss-roll tin and bake in a hot oven for approximately 30 minutes. Cut into fingers and dust with castor sugar.

COCONUT SNOWBALLS

$\frac{1}{2}$ *lb flour*   *4 oz margarine*
1 teaspoon baking powder   *2 oz castor sugar*
pinch of salt   *egg to mix*
dessicated coconut and raspberry jam to decorate

Sieve the flour, baking powder, and salt. Cut and rub in the margarine. Add the sugar and mix all to a very stiff dough using the beaten egg. Turn on to a floured board. Form into a log shape and cut into 14–16 portions. Shape into balls and place on a greased tray. Bake in a hot oven for 15 minutes, (7, F or 450°).

To finish, brush each little cake with hot raspberry jam and toss in coconut.

LITTLE APPLE CAKES

Probably of all the cakes made by this method I like these little apple cakes best. In appearance they remind me of queen cakes, and there should be no hint of the apple filling to be found inside.

8 oz flour   *4 oz margarine*
1 teaspoon cream of tartar   *4 oz sugar*
$\frac{1}{2}$ *teaspoon baking soda*   *1 egg*
a pinch of salt   *a little milk if necessary*
approx 1 cup stewed apple for the filling

Sieve the flour with the cream of tartar and the baking soda. Cut and rub in the margarine; add the sugar and mix all to a stiff dough with the beaten egg. The consistency is important and the dough should be as stiff as required for short crust pastry. Roll out to rather less than $\frac{1}{4}$-inch thick; cut into rounds and use half of these to line patty tins. Put a little stewed apple into each and cover with the remainder of the rounds of paste. It is worth noting that it is not necessary to damp the edges of the pastry for these little cakes. The top and bottom rounds seal naturally during the cooking. Bake in a hot oven for 15 minutes. Serve warm and dusted with icing sugar.

This quantity should make 18 small cakes.

FIG. 2.
(I) *Little Apple Cakes*—there should be no hint of the apple filling inside
(II) *Almond Buns*—a ball of almond paste lies hidden in each of these little buns

ALMOND BUNS

A ball of almond paste lies hidden in the centre of each of these little buns, making a pleasant surprise as well as contributing to their good eating qualities.

6 oz flour	*3 oz margarine*
a pinch of salt	*2 oz castor sugar*
½ teaspoon baking powder	*1 egg*

Almond paste :

2 oz ground almonds	*a little almond essence*
1 oz castor sugar	*approx ½ egg to bind*
1 oz icing sugar	

Flaked almonds to decorate

Sieve the flour, salt and baking powder together and cut and rub in the margarine. Add the castor sugar and bind all to a stiff paste with the beaten egg.

Next prepare the almond paste :—put the ground almonds, castor sugar and sieved icing sugar into a bowl. Flavour lightly with almond essence and mix all to a stiff paste with a little beaten egg. Then, using sugared hands, shape into 16 little balls.

Divide the dough into 16 even-sized pieces also, and flatten slightly with the hand. Place a ball of almond paste on each and draw the edges together. Mould into buns with the hand so that the almond mixture is completely enclosed. Turn the buns over, brush with egg and sprinkle with flaked almonds.

Bake in a fairly hot oven for approximately 15 minutes, suggested oven temperatures being 7, F or 450°.

And finally, a group of 3 small cakes, each different in its own way but all very similar to one another, except for the flavouring. They are simple and quick to produce being made like rock buns, while the recipe is so rich that they make very good eating. When baked they are split diagonally and filled with a suitably-flavoured butter icing. This makes them attractive to look at as well as moist and delicious.

Make them rich

COFFEE CREAM CAKES

6 oz flour

1 small teaspoon baking powder

a pinch of salt

3 oz margarine

2 oz castor sugar

1 egg

2 teaspoons coffee essence

Coffee butter icing:

1 oz margarine

2 oz icing sugar

coffee essence

Sieve the flour, baking powder and salt into a bowl and cut and rub in the margarine. Add the sugar and mix to a very stiff dough with the beaten egg and coffee essence. Arrange the mixture in 12 small rough heaps on a greased baking tray, and cook in a hot oven for 15 minutes, (7, F or 450°).

Meanwhile prepare the coffee butter icing by creaming the margarine, and gradually working in the other ingredients. Beat until very light.

When the cakes are cold, split diagonally and sandwich together again with the filling—it should show attractively. Dredge with icing sugar.

ORANGE CREAM CAKES

½ lb flour

1 teaspoon baking powder

a pinch of salt

4 oz margarine

3 oz sugar

1 egg to mix

the rind of one small orange

Filling:

1½ oz margarine

2 oz icing sugar

1 dessertspoonful ground almonds

orange rind to flavour

1 tablespoon orange juice

a little peach colouring

Sieve the dry ingredients and cut and rub in the margarine. Add the sugar and the grated orange rind. Mix to a stiff dough with beaten egg, and using a little milk in

29

addition, if necessary. Put the mixture out in small, rough heaps on to a greased tray. There should be approximately 16. Bake in a hot oven for 15 minutes.

While the cakes are cooking prepare the filling :—cream the margarine and gradually work in the sieved icing sugar and the other ingredients. Colour a pretty peach. Cut the cakes in two diagonally and spread with the filling. Put together again and dust with icing sugar.

COCONUT CREAM CAKES

½ *lb flour*	2½ *oz coconut*
1 *teaspoon baking powder*	1 *egg*
a pinch of salt	*a little vanilla essence*
4 *oz margarine*	*some milk to mix*
3 *oz castor sugar*	

Filling :

1½ *oz margarine*	*vanilla essence*
2½ *oz icing sugar*	*few drops of carmine*

Sieve the flour, baking powder and salt. Cut and rub in the margarine. Add the sugar and coconut. Beat the egg and add the vanilla essence. Use to mix all to a very stiff dough, adding milk if necessary. Put out in small rough heaps on to a greased tray, and bake in a hot oven for 15 minutes (7, F or 450°).

Make the filling by creaming the margarine and gradually beating in the sieved icing sugar. Flavour with vanilla, and colour delicately with carmine.

When the cakes are cold, split diagonally and sandwich together again with the filling, arranging it so that it shows attractively. Dust with icing sugar.

THE ART OF MAKING A SPONGE

A SPONGE cake is very good eating and the art of making it is not difficult to acquire. Indeed, I personally find it an easier mixture to prepare than a butter sponge.

A SECRET WORTH KNOWING

A sponge, however, is not intended for storing and is at its best for only a day or two. If you wish it to keep pleasantly moist for longer then try adding a dessertspoonful of glycerine at the same time as the flour. This makes a remarkable difference to the cake, and is well worth trying. Indeed the result is somewhat similar to a Genoese sponge, and to me at any rate, a well-made Genoese constitutes the peak of perfection in sponge cake.

A MATTER OF METHOD

There are at least three accepted methods of beating the eggs for a sponge, and while all are good, some find one easier than another:—

1. With this method the eggs and sugar are combined in a bowl and beaten together for 15–20 minutes until they are thick, creamy in colour, and light. Sometimes the process is hastened if the basin is placed over a pan of hot water. The gentle heat cooks the mixture slightly so that it thickens more quickly.

2. In the second method the yolks and the sugar are whisked until thick and creamy and the stiffly beaten whites are then folded in before the addition of the flour.

3. The last method is my own favourite:—separate the yolks from the whites, keeping the yolks in the half egg shell. Whip the whites until stiff and gradually whisk in the sugar and yolks, adding them alternately, and beating well between each addition.

A SPONGE SANDWICH

It is useful to remember when making a sponge mixture that it is usual to allow $1-1\frac{1}{2}$ oz of flour and sugar to each egg. No baking powder is required as a rule, except perhaps for Swiss rolls and Devonshire creams.

4 eggs	*a pinch of salt*
4 oz castor sugar	*a little grated lemon rind if wished*
4 oz flour	

Separate the whites from the yolks, keeping the yolks in the broken shells. Add a pinch of salt to the former and whisk until stiff. Then gradually beat in the sugar and yolks adding each alternately and beating well between each addition. Continue the beating until the mixture is light and thick. It is now ready for the addition of the flour and this process is most important. Sift the flour on to the eggs and at the same time fold it in, using a metal spoon. Turn the mixture into two prepared sandwich tins and bake in a moderately hot oven for approximately 20 minutes. The mixture will be firm to the touch, and show signs of shrinking from the edge of the tin when it is ready.

Baking temperatures are as follows:—gas ovens 5, E; electric ovens 400°.

Remember, too, that the cake will have a more attractive skin if the tin has been both greased and dusted with equal quantities of sugar and flour. If the sponge is to be served plain it is good to sprinkle the top with sugar before baking.

LESS ORTHODOX

The above recipe is the standard one but the two which follow do not conform to the conventional pattern. While unorthodox, they are both excellent. They are not so easy to make, however, and are only for those accomplished in the art of baking. I believe, nevertheless, that you will like both recipes very much.

A MOIST SPONGE CAKE

The proportion of hot milk which is incorporated with the flour gives this sponge its characteristic texture. You will find it attractively moist and a cake which will store better than the average sponge.

The art of making a sponge

3 eggs

6 oz castor sugar

1 teacup flour

6 dessertspoons hot milk

$\frac{1}{8}$ teaspoon baking powder

Separate the yolks from the whites of eggs. Add a pinch of salt to the latter and whisk until stiff. Next beat in the yolks and the sugar, adding these alternately. Meanwhile, measure the milk into a small saucepan and heat to just under boiling point. Sift the flour and baking powder on to the eggs and carefully fold in. At the same time gradually add the milk. Turn the mixture into a prepared cake tin and bake in a moderately-heated oven about 45 minutes, or until firm to the touch and beginning to shrink from the sides of the tin.

Split and fill as required.

A VERY LIGHT SPONGE CAKE

The small amount of flour used in the following recipe, in proportion to sugar, probably accounts for the very light texture of the cake. It is so light that it is important not to move it during the baking process or it may fall in the centre.

3 eggs

5 oz castor sugar

3 oz flour

Separate the yolks from the whites of egg. Add a pinch of salt to the latter and whisk until stiff. Place the bowl over a pan of hot, but not boiling, water and gradually beat in the yolks and the sugar. After the last of the sugar has been incorporated continue whisking for a further 4 minutes. Remove the whisk. Sift in the flour and, using an iron spoon, carefully fold into the egg mixture. Turn into a prepared cake tin and bake in a moderately-heated oven for approximately 45 minutes. (5, E or 400°).

A GENOESE SPONGE

A Genoese sponge keeps very well because of the melted butter which is folded in with the flour. This process requires deftness otherwise the cake mixture loses its light character before it is even put into the oven. To be able to make a good Genoese, however, is something of which to be proud.

4 eggs	*3 oz flour*
4 oz castor sugar	*3 oz melted butter*

Beat the eggs and sugar over hot, but not boiling, water until light and thick. Meanwhile melt the butter over a gentle heat, being careful not to make it hot.

Take the basin from the heat and whisk a few minutes longer. Sieve half the flour on top of the eggs and lightly fold into the mixture, at the same time adding the melted butter gradually. Repeat, being very careful not to over-stir the mixture as this will cause it to fall. There is also danger of the butter settling to the bottom of the bowl, so make sure to draw the spoon completely through the mixture with each folding. Pour into a prepared 7-inch cake tin and bake in a moderate oven for 40–45 minutes.

If the Genoese is required for cutting into small cakes use $4\frac{1}{2}$ oz flour in the above mixture instead of 3 oz flour. This will give a firmer texture which is easier to handle. In this case too, bake the mixture in a Swiss roll tin.

FILLING A SPONGE SANDWICH CAKE

While sponge cake is good to eat quite plain, it may be filled in any way you wish and, next to whipped cream with home-made raspberry jam, I recommend the refreshing flavour of lemon curd.

For a more special cake a combination of chopped tinned pineapple and whipped cream is fresh and pleasant as a filling in the sponge. Alternatively the sponge may be baked in one large flat tin and the cream and pineapple used decoratively on top rather than as a filling. When made like this the cake is nicer to eat if it is first split and spread with raspberry jam.

Needless to say, when strawberries and raspberries are available in the summer, they can be used most effectively instead of pineapple.

LEMON CURD

1 lemon	*1 egg*
4 oz sugar	*1 oz margarine*
a pinch of cornflour	

Grate the lemon and squeeze the juice. Put into a saucepan with the sugar, corn-flour, margarine, and yolk of egg. Whip the white of egg until stiff and fold in; then cook over a gentle heat until boiling. Strangely enough, in spite of popular belief, this mixture will not curdle.

DEVONSHIRE CREAMS

Devonshire creams are made using a sponge mixture and, to be correct, they should be dropped in teaspoonfuls on a flat sheet for baking. If the mixture is creamy and thick they will hold their shape in a very attractive manner. Some cooks, however, have not the skill and confidence to do this and so, if wished, the sponge may be baked in shallow patty tins. This is fool-proof, but the cakes are more clumsy than those made by the former method. It is obvious, therefore, that it is of consequence to have a sponge mixture which is thick and creamy, and this is partly ensured by using the maximum amount of flour consistent with producing a spongy cake.

2 eggs
3 oz castor sugar
3 oz flour
whipped cream and raspberry jam to fill

¼ teaspoonful baking powder
a pinch of salt

Separate the whites from the yolks. Add a pinch of salt and whisk until very stiff. Gradually and alternately, whisk in the sugar and yolks. Continue beating until the mixture is a creamy colour, and thickens, so that it leaves a heavy trail. When this stage is reached remove the beater and gently sift in the flour and baking powder. Then, using a metal spoon, fold in the dry ingredients. Meanwhile, have 2 or 3 baking sheets prepared. These should be greased and dusted with flour. Drop the sponge mixture out in teaspoonfuls, allowing room for them to spread. Dust with sugar, and bake in a hot oven for 5–7 minutes (7, F or 450°).

When cold, sandwich with a little raspberry jam and whipped cream. Serve dusted with icing sugar.

A SWISS ROLL

3 eggs
4½ oz castor sugar
3 oz flour
hot jam or lemon curd to fill

½ teaspoon baking powder
1 tablespoon cold water

Prepare the sponge mixture by your favourite method and, when folding in the flour, add the water also. Spread the mixture in a lined and greased swiss-roll tin and bake in a hot oven (7, F or 475°) for approximately 12 minutes. Then turn out on to a sugared paper. Spread quickly with the hot jam and roll up tightly. Finish with the heel of the cake tucked neatly to the under side. Trim the ends and dust with sugar.

CHOCOLATE LOG CAKE

2 eggs	$\frac{1}{2}$ oz cocoa
3 oz castor sugar	$\frac{1}{2}$ teaspoon baking powder
2 oz flour	a few drops of vanilla essence
2 tablespoonfuls milk	

Chocolate butter icing:

4 oz margarine	2 oz melted chocolate
6 oz icing sugar	a few drops of vanilla essence

Prepare the sponge mixture in the usual way, folding in the cocoa, milk and vanilla essence at the same time as the flour. Spread in a lined and greased swiss-roll tin and bake in a hot oven (7, F or 475°) for approximately 8–10 minutes. Turn out on to a piece of lightly-floured paper and roll up without any filling. Leave for a few minutes then carefully unroll.

To finish the cake:—first make the chocolate butter icing using the creaming method. Spread some over the slab of cake when quite cold and roll up once more. Dust off any surplus flour. Then cover the cake with the remainder of the icing, roughing it up into peaks to simulate the bark. Trim the ends. If wished, a diagonal wedge may be cut from one end of the cake before it is iced. This piece can be placed at the side of the roll to give an even more realistic appearance.

DRESSING UP A SPONGE CAKE

A SPONGE can be used as the foundation for many interesting cakes, but undoubtedly my favourite is a sherry cake. You will find it, perhaps, a little extravagant but so good that this will be forgotten in your pleasure with the result.

A brief picture of the cake will not be out of place:—the basic cake is a sponge; this is sandwiched with a thin layer of almond macaroon and soaked with sherry. For icing the sides and top and for the filling also, a butter icing is required which has been flavoured with sherry. A finishing touch is given by using crushed macaroon to cover the sides and top. It requires little imagination to realise that the combination of macaroon, sherry and sponge is very good indeed.

SHERRY CAKE

The sponge:
  2 eggs　　　　　　　　　　　*a pinch of salt*
  3 oz sugar　　　　　　　　　*1 tablespoon of water*
  3 oz flour

The macaroon mixture:
  1½ whites of egg　　　　　　*4 oz castor sugar*
  3 oz ground almonds　　　　*a little almond essence*

The sherry icing:
  3 oz butter (or margarine)　　*½ wine-glass of sherry*
  4 oz icing sugar

Half a wine-glass of sherry to soak the cake and a little green nut and silver balls to decorate it.

Make the sponge in the usual way and bake in one cake tin rather than in two sandwich tins.

FIG. 3. *Sherry Cake.*
(I) Soak the sponge with sherry, being as generous as possible without making the cake sodden
(II) It requires little imagination to realise that the combination of macaroon,
sherry and sponge is very good to eat

Next prepare the macaroon mixture:—whip the $1\frac{1}{2}$ egg whites until stiff and then fold in the sugar, ground almonds and essence. Spread the mixture on a tin lined with oiled paper. Use a wet knife for this purpose, and spread about $\frac{1}{4}$-inch thick. The area of the macaroon mixture should be greater than the cake, so as to allow trimmings to crush for the outside.

Bake the macaroon in a moderate oven and, when set and golden, remove from the oven and cut a piece the exact size of the cake. Crumble the trimmings with the fingers and return to the oven. Dry until quite crisp, then crush with a rolling pin as you would bread raspings.

Finishing the cake:—make the butter icing by creaming the butter until light and then gradually beating in the sieved icing sugar together with the sherry, adding a little at a time, since it is apt to curdle the mixture.

Put a generous spreading of the icing on the portion of macaroon and sandwich with the cake: the piece of macaroon makes the base of the sherry cake. Next soak the sponge with sherry, being as generous as possible, without making the cake sodden. Spread the icing on the sides of the cake and roll it, as you work, in the crushed macaroon. Finally, spread the top of the cake with icing and cover, like the sides, with macaroon. Decorate simply, using a sprinkling of green nut and silver balls.

A VARIATION

For those who do not care for sherry, the same cake may be flavoured with coffee essence. Add the coffee to the sponge and to the butter icing and assemble the cake as described above. Once more the texture of the macaroon contrasts and combines with the coffee sponge, to give a truly lovely cake.

PRALINE CAKE

Crushed caramel and toasted almonds are the special feature of this praline cake. They are used to cover the cake and give it a most appetising appearance and a good flavour. Unfortunately the caramel is apt to go sticky if exposed to the air, so it is best to use this cake immediately or to keep it stored in an air-tight tin when not in use.

FIG. 4.

Praline Cake. Crushed caramel and toasted almonds make a delicious decoration for this cake

The cake :

    a 4-egg sponge sandwich

Butter icing :

    3 oz margarine   *a squeeze of lemon juice*
    6 oz icing sugar   *vanilla essence*

Caramel :

    4 oz granulated sugar   *a pinch of cream of tartar*
    a little water   *2 oz shredded toasted almonds*

First prepare the caramel:—put the sugar into a small but strong saucepan and add a little water. Stir over a gentle heat until dissolved, then add the cream of tartar and remove the spoon. Boil gently until a rich golden colour. Pour immediately on to a greased tin. When cold, crush with a rolling pin and mix with the toasted shredded almonds.

Now prepare the butter icing in the usual way and cream thoroughly to ensure a very light mixture. Use to sandwich the sponge.

Continue by spreading the butter icing over the sides of the cake and roll it, as you proceed, in the caramel mixture. Finally spread the top of the cake with the icing and sprinkle with caramel and almonds. No further decoration is required but sometimes the butter icing is coloured either pink or green.

LEMON SPONGE CAKE

The sponge:

3 eggs	*a pinch of salt*
6 oz castor sugar	*grated rind of $\frac{1}{2}$ a lemon*
$4\frac{1}{2}$ oz flour	

Filling:

$1\frac{1}{2}$ oz margarine	*2 oz icing sugar*
lemon curd to flavour	

Icing:

10 oz icing sugar	*boiling water*
a squeeze of lemon juice	*a spoonful of fine julienne strips cut from the zest of the lemon*

Make the sponge cake by your favourite method folding in the grated lemon rind with the flour. Turn into a 7-inch cake tin and bake in a moderate oven (6, D or 400°) for approximately 25 minutes.

When cold, split and fill with butter icing well flavoured with lemon curd. The cake is finally iced as follows:—peel off the zest of a lemon with a sharp knife and then cut diagonally into fine julienne strips. Cook these in boiling water until tender.

Sieve the icing sugar, add a squeeze of lemon juice and mix to a coating consistency with boiling water. Beat in the strips of lemon rind and use to coat the top and sides of the cake.

A FRENCH RUM CAKE

Basically this cake consists of a light sponge mixture baked so as to give a shallow single-deck cake. This is then soaked with a rum flavoured syrup and topped with whipped cream. Decorate if you wish with a sprinkling of toasted flaked almonds.

3 eggs	*a little grated lemon rind*
3 oz castor sugar	*3 oz flour*

Rum syrup:

1 breakfast cup of water	*rum to lace*
4 oz sugar	

Whipped cream, sweetened and flavoured with vanilla essence.
A few toasted flaked almonds to decorate.

Separate the yolks from the whites of eggs and whisk the whites until stiff. Then gradually and alternately, add the yolks and the castor sugar. Flavour with a little grated lemon rind and continue beating until thick and creamy. Remove the whisk, sift the flour lightly on to the egg mixture, folding it in at the same time with a tablespoon. Turn the mixture into a prepared 8-inch cake tin and bake in a moderate oven for approximately 20–25 minutes. Suggested oven temperatures being 6, E or 400°.

Now prepare the rum syrup:—put the water and sugar into a small saucepan and stir over a gentle heat until the sugar is dissolved. Remove the spoon and bring to the boil, then boil gently until a syrup is formed. Lace with rum and use to soak the cake.

Whip the cream, sweeten and flavour with vanilla and swirl attractively over the top of the cake. Sprinkle with toasted flaked almonds.

CARAMEL SPONGE CAKE

This type of sponge cake has a good flavour obtained by using finely-crushed caramel in addition to the usual sugar in the sponge mixture. Remember, however, the caramel must be really as fine as sugar before it is used, otherwise it shows as sticky, dark spots when the cake is baked. The rough pieces, which escape the pounding, may very well be kept for decorating the top of the cake later. The caramel should be a rich colour, otherwise it will not impart the required flavour and colour to the sponge.

Caramel:

   3 oz castor sugar

Sponge:

   3 eggs   *3 oz flour*
   3 oz castor sugar

Whipped cream, sweetened and flavoured with vanilla.
A few toasted flaked almonds to decorate.

Begin by making the caramel:—put the 3 oz castor sugar into a small, strong saucepan. No water is required. Heat gently until the sugar melts and gradually turns a rich caramel colour. Quickly pour on to an oiled tray and put aside to cool. When hard, crush as fine as possible. Those with a pestle and mortar should use this, others will find a rolling pin satisfactory.

Now prepare the sponge:—separate the yolks from the whites of egg and whisk the whites until stiff. Then gradually beat in the yolks, sugar and two-thirds of the crushed caramel, adding these alternately. Continue beating until the mixture is thick and the caramel dissolved. Lastly fold in the sifted flour and turn the mixture into a prepared 8-inch cake tin. Bake in a moderate oven for approximately 20–25 minutes. Suggested oven temperatures being 6, E or 400°.

To finish the cake:—swirl the top with sweetened and flavoured whipped cream. Decorate by sprinkling with the remainder of the crushed caramel and toasted flaked almonds.

LEMON CURD CAKE

   4 eggs   *4 oz flour*
   4 oz castor sugar

Filling:

   lemon curd

Royal icing:

4 oz icing sugar   *a little egg white*

Begin by making the sponge cake using your favourite method. Bake the mixture in two sandwich tins for approximately 20–25 minutes. Suggested oven temperatures being 6, E or 400°.

When cold, sandwich with the lemon curd.

Now prepare the royal icing:—sieve the icing sugar and mix to a stiff paste with a little white of egg. Beat well so that it will pipe easily. Transfer to a bag fitted with a fairly heavy star icing tube and pipe in the form of a trellis across the top of the cake. The lines should be about 3/4-inch apart. Pipe a star at each intersection and decorate with a silver ball. Pipe stars also round the edge of the cake. Finish the cake by filling lemon curd into each diamond made by the royal icing.

VARIATIONS OF A VICTORIA SANDWICH

A VICTORIA sandwich cake or a "butter sponge", as many call it, is undoubtedly a most useful form of cake and makes the basis of a great repertoire of others. It is a cake housewives take pride in making well, and they are often very critical of any faults. A good butter sponge should be light and moist, flat on top and an appealing golden colour. Quite a common fault is a cake which is not perfectly level. This is unsightly and may be extravagant if it is necessary to trim it. It is nearly always caused by having the oven too hot, perhaps in combination with a rather stiff batter. Again some cooks are irritated by a sandwich which is full of large holes or badly blistered on top. This fault is usually due to the excessive use of baking powder. Alternatively, a cake with a very close texture is disappointing and may be caused by any of the following:—insufficient creaming of the margarine and sugar, too vigorous beating of the batter when adding the flour, or too stiff a mixture.

HINTS FOR SUCCESS

A butter sponge is made by the basic method of creaming the margarine with the sugar until very light. Naturally this process is important and, in order to lessen the hard work involved, many warm the margarine first. Less obvious, yet equally important, is the temperature of the other ingredients, and for perfect results the eggs and flour should be at least at kitchen temperature. Eggs taken from a cold larder or refrigerator spoil many a cake. They make the mixture more liable to curdle and more diligent beating is required to obtain a light batter. It is, therefore, worthwhile putting the eggs and flour in a warm place prior to making a cake. Put them for example on the plate rack of a gas cooker or in the warming cupboard of an electric stove. I am convinced you will find this a good idea.

VICTORIA SANDWICH

6 oz margarine	*3 eggs*
6 oz castor sugar	*1 teaspoon baking powder*
7 oz flour	*flavouring if wished;*
	e. g. vanilla essence, or a grating
	of lemon

Cream the margarine and sugar very thoroughly. Next add the well-whisked eggs by degrees, beating well between each addition. Lastly add the flour and baking powder, stirring them in lightly, and adding roughly one-third at a time.

Divide the mixture between two lined and greased sandwich tins. Spread evenly and bake in a moderate oven for approximately 30 minutes.

The exact oven temperatures are as follows:—gas Ovens 5 or E electric Ovens 400°.

When cold, fill as wished with raspberry jam, lemon curd, or a butter icing.

AN ALMOND SANDWICH CAKE

It is not generally known, perhaps, that marzipan combines very nicely with a butter sponge and a pleasant sandwich cake is made as follows:—

Make 4 oz of ground almonds into marzipan and colour it pink. Cut in two and roll out half to use as a filling for the cake. Stick all together with a spreading of apricot or raspberry jam. Next cover the top with a thin layer of almond paste and ice the cake all over with 10 oz of white water icing. The result is quite effective since the pink of the marzipan will shine through the water icing. Decorate as you please, perhaps with almonds and silver balls.

RUSSIAN CAKE

Russian cake is another version of the Victoria sandwich in which the combination of marzipan and a butter sponge is used to advantage.

A Russian cake has many points in its favour. It is most attractive to look at, delicious to eat, while it keeps nicely for a matter of a week or so. Besides it cuts into a surprising number of slices and is therefore most useful when special catering is being planned.

Variations of a Victoria sandwich

The cake I think of as Russian cake is also known by the name Battenburg or chapel window cake. Chapel window cake is certainly very descriptive, for the distinctive feature of this cake is the chess-board effect obtained by using cake of two colours. Pink and natural colours are usual but sometimes chocolate is used instead of the pink.

A special cake tin is really necessary when making Russian cake and the standard one measures 9 by 6 inches and has a detachable division down the centre.

The cake mixture :

4 oz margarine	*2 eggs*
4 oz sugar	*1 teaspoon baking powder*
4½ oz flour	*apricot jam*

The almond paste :

6 oz ground almonds	*egg to bind*
2 oz castor sugar	*a little almond essence*
4 oz icing sugar	

Prepare the cake tin first by lining the bottom of each half with paper and then greasing.

Next cream the margarine and sugar thoroughly. Gradually beat in the well-whisked eggs and lastly, lightly beat in the flour and baking powder. Spread half the mixture into one side of the cake tin and colour the other half pink. Spread in the cake tin and bake in a moderate oven for 30 minutes (5, E or 400°).

Icing the Russian Cake :—cut the two strips into 4 long bars—2 pink and 2 natural colour. Spread with apricot jam and re-assemble to give the chess-board effect.

Next prepare the almond paste :—sieve the icing sugar and combine with the ground almonds and castor sugar. Add a little almond essence and mix to a stiff paste with beaten egg.

Now take the dimensions of the cake by measuring the length and circumference with pieces of string and roll the marzipan to the correct size. Spread it with jam and place the cake along the centre. Carefully envelop it in the marzipan, easing it round the corners and pinching the join away with the fingers. Lastly, decorate the four edges by pinching with the fingers in the way shortbread is often finished; trim the ends. Sometimes, too, the top of the cake is decorated further perhaps with cherry and angelica.

47

ORANGE CAKE

The filling and icing used in the following recipe for orange cake have a particularly fine, fresh-fruit flavour, while the icing is a pretty soft shade due to the orange juice which is used in the making.

5 oz margarine	*2 eggs*
5 oz sugar	*rind of one orange*
5 oz flour	*a little orange juice*
½ teaspoon baking powder	

Orange filling:

1 yolk of a hard-boiled egg	*1½ oz icing sugar*
1 oz ground almonds	*1 oz margarine*
rind of orange	*a little orange juice*

Orange water icing:

4 oz icing sugar	*juice of one orange*

Prepare the cake as follows:—cream the margarine and sugar until very light. Grate in the rind of the orange and beat in the lightly-whisked eggs. Lastly add the flour and baking powder, using a little orange juice to keep the batter light. Spread the mixture in two prepared sandwich tins and bake in a moderate oven for approximately 30 minutes.

When the cake is cold, prepare the filling:—sieve the hard-boiled egg yolk; cream the margarine and gradually beat in the sugar, prepared yolk, ground almonds and orange rind. Finally add sufficient juice to make all a good spreading consistency. Use to sandwich the cake.

Make the icing next:—bring the orange juice to the boil and use to mix the sugar to an easy-to-spread consistency. Use immediately, spreading over the top of the cake with a hot knife.

A more elaborate cake may be made by making double quantity of the filling and using a proportion to spread on the sides of the cake. These should then be rolled in shredded toasted almonds or toasted coconut: either of these will give the cake a really luxury appearance and flavour. The top, too, may be piped to your fancy, with butter icing, or is pleasant decorated with thin slices of citron peel and cherries.

WALNUT CAKE

Walnut cake is good for cutting, and is generally liked on account of its flavour and the white icing with which it is usually covered. Sometimes, as in the recipe which follows, this is a simple water icing but experts often prefer to use American icing. The recipe for this is given in another part of the book; half quantities should be made and used at a coating consistency *(see page 180)*.

3 oz margarine	*½ gill milk*
4 oz castor sugar	*½ level teaspoon baking soda*
2 eggs	*1 level teaspoon cream of tartar*
6 oz flour	*1 oz chopped walnuts*

Filling:

1½ oz margarine	*a little vanilla essence*
3 oz icing sugar	*1 tablespoon cream if possible*
½ oz walnuts	

Icing:

10 oz icing sugar	*boiling water to mix*
5 half walnuts to decorate	

Make the cake using the creaming method:—cream the margarine and sugar well and then beat in the well-whisked eggs. Next, lightly beat in the flour and raising agents alternately with the milk and lastly stir in the chopped walnuts. Divide the mixture between two prepared sandwich tins and bake in a moderate oven for approximately 20–30 minutes.

To finish:—make the filling by creaming the margarine and gradually beating in the sieved icing sugar, the cream and the chopped walnuts. Use to sandwich the cake. Make up the water icing in the usual way and use to cover the cake. Decorate with half-walnuts.

Note. When using walnuts it is often necessary to freshen them first by placing in a moderately heated oven for a few minutes.

FIG. 5. *Marshmallow Cake.*
(I) While the cake is hot from the oven the top is covered with
halved marshmallow sweets
(II) May be iced with chocolate water icing, while toasted whole almonds
make an effective decoration. Allow one to each "scallop" made by the marshmallows

(III) *Marshmallow Cake* a trick of the kitchen

MARSHMALLOW CAKE

A marshmallow cake is very amusing to make and will always prove a "talking piece" at any tea-table. At the same time it is simple to prepare and its interesting feature really amounts to a trick of the kitchen—easy to accomplish when one knows how.

In the first place a shallow cake is baked and when it is taken from the oven the top is covered with halved marshmallow sweets. These are closely packed and placed sticky side down. The heat from the cake causes them to melt slightly so that they merge together and stick to the top. To prevent them perhaps slipping off the cake it should be left in the tin at this stage, and indeed, until it is cold. Finally the cake is split and filled with lemon curd, then covered with a lemon water icing. Incidentally the cake has a pretty scalloped edge due to the marshmallow hidden under the icing.

3 oz margarine	*½ teaspoon baking powder*
3 oz castor sugar	*2 eggs*
3½ oz flour	

51

lemon curd to fill
approx 4 oz round marshmallow sweets

Water icing:

8 oz icing sugar   *boiling water to mix*
a squeeze of lemon juice

Prepare the cake as follows:—cream the margarine and sugar thoroughly. Gradually beat in the whisked egg and lastly add the flour and baking powder. Turn the mixture into a prepared 6-inch cake tin—it is best to have the sides lined with paper for this cake. Bake in a moderately heated oven for 30–35 minutes (5, D or 400°).

While the cake is in the oven cut the marshmallows in two, using a pair of scissors, and immediately it is baked arrange these to cover the top closely. They should be placed in position cut-side down. Press home with the fingers and put aside to cool.

Turn the cake out of the tin, remove the paper, split and fill with the lemon curd. Spread a little lemon curd over the top of the cake too, using just sufficient to fill any chinks between the sweets. Finally make the water icing and use to coat the cake. For decoration I generally use whole cherries rolled in granulated sugar.

If a chocolate flavour is preferred the marshmallow cake may be filled instead with chocolate butter icing, also to fill the chinks between the marshmallows, and the whole coated with chocolate water icing. In this case I use toasted whole almonds as a simple but pleasing decoration. These are arranged in a circle round the edge of the cake, allowing one to each "scallop" made by a marshmallow sweet.

CHERRY AND WALNUT SANDWICH CAKE

6 oz margarine   *1 teaspoon baking powder*
6 oz castor sugar   *2 oz glacé cherries (quartered)*
3 eggs   *2 oz walnuts (chopped)*
7 oz flour   *a little vanilla essence*

Filling:

1½ oz margarine   *1 tablespoon cream*
3 oz icing sugar   *a little vanilla essence*

52

Variations of a Victoria sandwich

Water icing for the top of the cake :

5 oz icing sugar   boiling water to mix

Cream the margarine and sugar thoroughly and then gradually beat in the lightly-whisked eggs. With the last of the egg add the flour and baking powder and finally stir in the cherries, walnuts and vanilla essence. Divide the mixture between two prepared sandwich tins and bake in a moderate oven for 20–30 minutes.

To finish :—make the filling by creaming the margarine and gradually beating in the sieved icing sugar, the cream and the vanilla essence. Use to sandwich the cake. Make up the water icing in the usual way and use to cover the top of the cake. Decorate with a few half walnuts and whole cherries.

FAVOURITE CHOCOLATE CAKES

CHOCOLATE cake for tea is always a popular choice—dark, glossy and luscious with icing—and the recipes for this type of cake are numerous. They range from a simple sponge or butter sandwich to the most exciting of all—a Clifton cake. This is one of my favourites and, in my own home, it is often baked when special guests are to be honoured.

FLAVOURING THE CHOCOLATE CAKE

Chocolate cakes may either be flavoured with a good quality cocoa or a dark block chocolate and frequently it is an improvement to add a little vanilla essence to the mixture to bring out the chocolate flavouring. The best way to melt chocolate for use in cakes is to break it into cubes, put it into a small bowl and place the bowl over a pan of hot water. Given plenty of time, you will find the chocolate melts to a thick cream when it is stirred. Avoid over-heating chocolate as this spoils the flavour; neither is it necessary to grate it or add water. In fact the addition of water, even a drop, thickens it in a curious way.

CHOCOLATE SPONGE SANDWICH

3 eggs	*2 tablespoons milk*
4 oz sugar	*a pinch of salt*
3 oz flour	*½ teaspoon baking powder*
¾ oz cocoa	*a little vanilla essence*

Blend the cocoa with the milk. Separate the yolks from the whites of egg. Add a pinch of salt to the whites, and whisk up stiffly. Gradually beat in the sugar and yolks adding these alternately and whisking well between each addition. If this is done correctly the mixture should remain thick and spongy. The process will take about 15 minutes.

Lastly, fold in the flour, baking powder, vanilla, cocoa and milk. This should be done with a tablespoon and the mixture should be turned over and over very lightly until completely mixed. Divide between two sandwich tins and bake in a moderately hot oven for 20–30 minutes (6, E or 400°). The sandwich tins should be prepared by lining the bottom with a piece of paper, greasing and dusting with flour. This gives the cake a good skin.

This sandwich is good filled with whipped cream and the top should be dusted thickly with icing sugar.

A STANDARD CHOCOLATE CAKE

Butter sponge :

4 oz margarine	*5 oz flour*
4 oz castor sugar	*1 teaspoon baking powder*
3–4 eggs	*a little vanilla essence*
4 oz powdered drinking chocolate	

Filling :

1 oz margarine	*1/2 oz chocolate*
1 1/2 oz icing sugar	

Icing :

8 oz icing sugar	*a speck of butter*
3 oz chocolate	*boiling water to mix*

Cream the margarine and sugar until light and creamy. Then beat in the well-whisked eggs. With the last of the egg add the chocolate, flour, baking powder and vanilla. Divide the mixture between two prepared sandwich tins and bake in a moderate oven (5, D or 400°) for approximately 30 minutes.

When cold, fill with the chocolate-flavoured butter icing and coat the top and sides with the water icing. The cake may be decorated with nuts or by piping with a little of the butter icing.

CHOCOLATE SANDWICH CAKE

The following recipe for chocolate cake is economical but surprisingly good.

3 oz margarine	*1 oz cocoa*
3 oz sugar	*small ½ teaspoon baking soda*
5 oz flour	*1 teaspoon baking powder*
1 egg	*a little vanilla essence*
1 tablespoon syrup	*rather more than 1 gill buttermilk*
	or sour milk

Chocolate butter icing :

3 oz margarine	*3 oz melted chocolate*
3 oz icing sugar	*vanilla essence*

Chocolate water icing :

4 oz icing sugar	*a speck of butter*
2 oz chocolate	*boiling water*
3 oz toasted almonds to finish the sides of the cake	

Cream the margarine and sugar thoroughly. Beat in the golden syrup and the lightly-whisked egg. Then add the dry ingredients alternately with the buttermilk keeping the mixture slack. Divide between two sandwich tins and bake in a moderate oven for approximately 25 minutes (5, D or 400°).

When cold finish as follows :—prepare the chocolate butter icing in the usual way and use to sandwich the cake. Spread also on the sides and roll the cake in the toasted shredded almonds.

Lastly spread the top with the chocolate water icing.

A few chocolate truffles make a simple and effective decoration for this cake.

Note. A speck of butter is often added to chocolate water icing to make it glossy. Thorough beating also has this effect.

A "SPANISH" CHOCOLATE CAKE

The recipe for this luscious chocolate cake was given to me by a friend who lived in Barcelona and, for this reason, I have always distinguished it from the others by calling it a "Spanish" Chocolate Cake.

The recipe is curious in that it calls for very little flour—only 1 oz to approximately 4 oz of margarine and sugar. For this reason the mixture is apt to subside sadly while the cake is in the oven. However, knowing this is likely to happen, the cook can proceed in confidence for the cake has excellent eating qualities, with a true chocolate flavour.

2 eggs and equal their weight in sugar, margarine and dark chocolate
1 oz flour   *$^3/_4$ oz shredded almonds*

Melt the chocolate. Put the margarine in a saucepan and melt over a gentle heat. As it melts, pour it off on to the chocolate and stir it in. Next stir in the 2 yolks, the flour and sugar, and lastly fold in the stiffly-beaten whites. Pour the mixture into a tin measuring 9 by 6 inches. Sprinkle with shredded almonds and bake in a moderate oven for approximately 40 minutes (5, D or 400°). Avoid disturbing the cake during this period. Cool the cake in the tin and when cold cut into fingers.

Note. A standard Russian cake tin is the correct size for this mixture.

CHOCOLATE CHIP CAKE

The special feature of this cake is the chocolate which, in this case, is added to the mixture in rough pieces. It melts slightly during the baking, and is a pleasant surprise when the cake is cut.

6 oz margarine   *1 teaspoon baking powder*
6 oz castor sugar   *4 oz dark chocolate chopped into*
3 eggs   *pieces the size of a pea*
7 oz flour   *$^1/_2$ teaspoon vanilla essence*

Cream the margarine and sugar thoroughly. Gradually beat in the lightly-whisked eggs and stir in the flour and baking powder in two or three amounts. With the last of the flour add the broken chocolate and vanilla essence. Divide between two prepared sandwich tins and bake in a moderate oven for approximately 30 minutes.

When cold, sandwich with chocolate butter icing and coat with a chocolate water icing. A suitable, yet simple decoration can be obtained by sticking chocolate dragees round the edges.

CHOCOLATE ORANGE CAKE

Chocolate orange cake is one of the most delicious and attractive cakes I know. In the first place a brief description will not be out of place since the cake is unusual and perhaps a little elaborate to make.

The basic cake is an orange-flavoured butter sandwich, and the filling consists of marzipan made into a spreading consistency with orange juice flavoured with orange rind, coloured a pretty shade of green. There are three layers of this pleasant filling and you can imagine that a cross-section of the cake looks very well indeed. The whole is iced with chocolate water icing and decorated with balls of marzipan coloured to match the filling. Those who are expert at piping might like to pipe these with a whirling line of chocolate water icing before putting them on the cake. The result is delightful and the cake excellent to eat.

Ingredients for the Cake :

6 oz margarine	3 eggs
6 oz sugar	1 teaspoonful baking powder
6 oz flour	rind of one orange

Filling :

3 oz ground almonds	a little orange rind
3 oz icing sugar	orange juice to mix
green colouring	

Chocolate icing :

6 oz icing sugar	a speck of butter
3 oz dark chocolate	boiling water to mix

Marzipan balls :

1 tablespoonful ground almonds	green colouring
1 tablespoonful icing sugar	orange juice to mix

Prepare the cake first :—cream the margarine and sugar very thoroughly. Gradually beat in the well whisked eggs and lastly add the orange rind, flour and baking powder. Divide between two prepared sandwich tins and bake in a moderate oven for 25–30 minutes (5, D or 400°).

FIG. 6. *Chocolate Orange Cake.*
(I) Balls of green marzipan, piped with a whirling line of chocolate icing, decorate this excellent
cake
(II) The three layers of filling are coloured green to match the marzipan balls decorating
the cake

When the cake is cold prepare the filling :—sieve the icing sugar and combine with the ground almonds. Flavour with orange rind and mix to a spreading consistency with orange juice. Colour a pretty green.

Split each half of the sandwich cake and spread with the filling. Re-assemble the cake so that there are three layers of filling and four of cake. Place on an upturned plate preparatory to icing.

Next prepare the water icing :—sieve the icing sugar and melt the chocolate. Combine these, add a speck of butter and sufficient boiling water to mix all to a spreading consistency. Use quickly to cover the top and sides of the cake. Spread neatly with a knife dipped in hot water. When making chocolate icing it is always important to remember that it sets quickly and that, therefore, the initial consistency should be softer than for other types of water icing. To get a perfect surface use a knife which is hot but not wet for spreading.

The decoration :—to decorate this cake have 5 or 6 balls made from green marzipan, mixed to match the filling. These balls should be about the size of marbles; one is placed in the centre of the cake and the remaining 4 or 5 round the edge.

If you are prepared to take a little trouble the balls look better piped with a spiral line of chocolate icing. To do this put a little of the chocolate icing in a paper icing bag as soon as it is mixed. No pipe is required. When the cake is iced pipe the marzipan balls, snipping sufficient from the point of the bag to allow a light line of icing to come through. Pipe quickly, starting in the centre of each ball and then round and round. Indeed, I know a little boy who calls this a "whirligig cake".

CLIFTON CAKE

Clifton cake should always be made a little in advance of the date of cutting if it is to be enjoyed at its best. This can well be understood when it is realised that the basic mixture is more in the form of a biscuit than a true cake batter, and it is necessary to allow it time to soften and mellow in its contact with the chocolate icing.

4 oz margarine	*¼ teaspooon baking powder*
3 oz castor sugar	*1 yolk of egg*
2 oz shelled Brazil nuts	*1 teaspoon coffee essence*
3 oz ground almonds	*pinch of salt*
2 oz flour	

Chocolate butter icing:

> 3 oz margarine   2 oz dark chocolate
>
> 4 oz icing sugar

Decoration:

> 1–2 tablespoons coarsely-grated chocolate
>
> shredded almonds or chocolate vermicelli
>
> a little green cake decoration

Grind the shelled Brazil nuts in a nut mill. Put the sugar, ground nuts, flour, baking powder and salt into a bowl and rub in the margarine. Add the coffee essence and yolk of egg and mix to a stiff paste. If necessary put aside to firm a little. Turn on to a floured board, cut in three and roll or pat each piece to fit a 6-inch sandwich tin. The mixture should be approximately $\frac{1}{4}$-inch thick in the tins. It is best to grease these tins and to line the bottom with paper.

Bake in a moderate oven for approximately $\frac{1}{2}$ an hour (5, D or 400°).

The cake is now ready for icing but this is best postponed for 3 or 4 days to allow time for it to soften. With this in view it should not be put in a tin but rather left on a plate in a cupboard.

Next the icing:—cream the margarine and gradually beat in the sieved icing sugar. Melt the chocolate over warm water and add this also. Beat thoroughly.

Use this butter icing to sandwich the three pieces of cake. Spread the butter icing evenly round the sides of the cake and roll in toasted shredded almonds or chocolate vermicelli. Spread the icing over the top of the cake also and cover with the coarsely-grated chocolate. Decorate with a little green vermicelli. Store in a tin for a few days before cutting.

Clifton cake may also be made using coffee butter icing instead of chocolate.

BELGIAN CHOCOLATE CAKE
rich and delicious

> 8 oz dark chocolate   2 eggs
>
> 8 oz margarine   a little vanilla essence
>
> 8 oz plain sweet biscuits $\frac{1}{2}$ oz shredded almonds or chopped
>
> 2 level dessertspoons sugar   walnuts

Melt the chocolate and the margarine separately. Meanwhile beat the eggs and the sugar together. Have the melted margarine hot and add quickly; this should have the effect of partly cooking the eggs so that the mixture resembles lemon curd—if necessary return all to the saucepan and cook over a gentle heat for a few minutes. Next add the melted chocolate gradually and lastly the vanilla essence and the broken biscuits. Press into a greased and lined tin measuring 9 by 6 inches. Sprinkle with toasted nuts and put in a cool place to set. Cut into fingers for serving.

CHOCOLATE CAKE WITH FUDGE ICING

6 oz margarine	*1½ oz ground almonds*
6 oz sugar	*6 oz powdered drinking chocolate*
5–6 eggs	*¾ teaspoon baking powder*
6 oz flour	*½ teaspoon vanilla essence*

Fudge icing :

2 oz margarine	*2 oz dark chocolate*
1 small tin evaporated milk	*vanilla essence*
6 oz granulated sugar	*½ oz chopped walnuts*

Cream the margarine and sugar until light. Gradually beat in the lightly-whisked eggs and, with the last of the egg, the dry ingredients. Turn the mixture into a lined 8-inch cake tin and bake in a moderate oven for approximately 1 hour. Suggested oven temperatures being 4 or D—C or 350°.

When the cake is taken from the oven do not remove the paper since this will later hold the fudge icing until it sets.

To make the fudge icing :—melt the margarine in a small, strong saucepan. Add the tinned milk and the sugar. Stir over a gentle heat until the sugar is dissolved then bring to the boil. Simmer gently, still stirring, until a little gives a "soft ball", when tested in cold water. Add the melted chocolate and the vanilla essence and beat until the fudge shows signs of thickening. Then pour quickly over the cake leaving the surface in attractive swirls. Sprinkle with chopped walnuts. Once the fudge has set the paper may be removed.

FAVOURITE COFFEE CAKES

COFFEE probably ranks on a par with chocolate as a favourite flavour for cakes and it scores in at least two respects; it is easier and cheaper to use. Often, however, the two flavourings combine well together, as in the first recipe, in which chocolate truffles are used as the decoration for this attractive coffee cake.

COFFEE TRUFFLE CAKE

6 oz margarine
6 oz castor sugar
7 oz flour

3 eggs
1 teaspoon baking powder
coffee essence to flavour

Filling:

1½ oz margarine
3 oz icing sugar

1 tablespoon cream
coffee essence to flavour

Icing:

10 oz icing sugar
boiling water

coffee essence to flavour

Decoration:

5 chocolate truffles (or hazelnuts)

Cream the margarine and sugar together until very light. Then gradually beat in the whisked eggs. Add the coffee essence and lastly stir in the flour and baking powder. Divide the mixture between two prepared sandwich tins and bake in a moderate oven for approximately 30 minutes (5, D or 400°).

When cold, sandwich together with the coffee butter filling and ice the top and sides of the cake with the coffee water icing.

Decorate, simply and effectively, by placing the five chocolate truffles around the edge of the cake.

These may either be purchased in a sweet shop or made at home. A few can easily be concocted for the purpose as follows:—melt a little chocolate in a bowl placed over a pan of hot water—about 2 oz chocolate will be sufficient. Flavour with coffee essence; the addition of this will thicken the chocolate surprisingly. Then add sufficient ground almonds to make the mixture stiff enough to handle with ease. Shape into small balls and toss in chocolate vermicelli.

Alternatively, whole hazelnuts may be used, and these make a quick and pleasing decoration.

COFFEE MERINGUE CAKE

Coffee meringue cake consists basically of four thin rounds of meringue. When baked these are sandwiched together with a delicious coffee butter cream, and this mixture is also used to cover the top and sides of the cake. The whole is decorated lavishly with toasted almonds and the combination is very good to eat.

Your immediate reaction I am sure, will be, that such a cake might be difficult to cut but, surprisingly enough, this is not so. A meringue cake should be made several days before it is required and during this period it will soften sufficiently to slice perfectly.

I like to serve this cake in generous pieces and always with a plate and fork, otherwise it is difficult to eat. A meringue cake may also be served as a sweet with, perhaps, a portion of whipped cream.

Ingredients for the meringue:

4 whites of egg   a pinch of salt
8½ oz castor sugar

Cover four baking sheets with greaseproof paper and draw a circle on each, using a round sandwich tin or large saucepan lid as a guide, and grease. Next add a pinch of salt to the four whites of egg and whisk until very stiff. Whisk in a teaspoonful of the sugar and lightly fold in the remainder. Divide the meringue out on to the four prepared trays and spread neatly and evenly to give the circular shape. The meringue should be rather more than a ¼-inch thick. Dust with castor sugar and bake as for meringue in a gently-heated oven until golden and crisp. The time taken will be approximately one hour.

The greatest difficulty likely to be encountered in the baking of the meringue cake will be in the arrangement of the four trays in the oven. Most ovens are fitted with only three shelves designed to take one tray each; this leaves us with the awkward problem of what to do with the fourth round of meringue. A little ingenuity, however, will solve this difficulty and I contrive to accommodate the last baking sheet by placing it on an upturned cake tin on the floor of the oven.

Icing the coffee meringue cake :—

Coffee crème au beurre :

3 oz granulated sugar	*8 oz butter*
6 tablespoons water	*coffee essence to flavour*
3 egg yolks	

Put the sugar and water into a small saucepan and stir over a gentle heat until dissolved. Remove the spoon and bring to the boil; boil gently until 216° or until a little, when tested in cold water, will form a "thread" between the finger and thumb.

Meanwhile have the egg yolks in a bowl and beaten into a cream with a whisk. Gradually pour on the hot syrup, beating all the time, and continue whisking until the mixture is thick and light.

Now cream the butter and gradually beat in the egg mixture. Flavour with coffee essence.

Having prepared the filling, toast 6 oz flaked almonds and set aside to cool.

Use the coffee crème au beurre to sandwich the four circles of meringue together. Then, if the cake is not sufficiently neat, trim a little round the sides and spread with the icing. Roll carefully in the flaked almonds. Cover the top of the cake in the same way and finish with a generous sprinkling of nuts.

*The prettiest finish for this cake is simple and effective :—*cut 4 or 5 strips of greaseproof paper about 1-inch wide, and space out neatly on top of the cake. Then dust over these with a generous shower of icing sugar; remove carefully and you will be pleased and surprised at the attractive appearance this gives the cake.

Incidentally I like to serve this cake on a silver cake board or tray, rather than on a cake plate.

*Note :—*Toasted coconut may be used instead of almonds if wished, while a good alternative flavour to the coffee essence used in the butter icing, is lemon flavouring added in the form of lemon curd.

BRANDY SNAP CAKE

A combination of brandy snaps and coffee can make an exciting gateau suitable for party catering. The basic cake is a coffee-flavoured butter sponge and the decoration consists of horn-shaped brandy snaps arranged spoke fashion around the top of the cake. For preference I make this cake in a ring tin, though this is by no means essential.

4 oz margarine	*2 eggs*
4 oz castor sugar	*1 small teaspoon baking powder*
4½ oz flour	*coffee essence to flavour*

Coffee butter icing:

4 oz margarine	*1 tablespoon cream*
6 oz icing sugar	*coffee essence to flavour*

Decoration:

approx 16–20 horn-shaped brandy snaps
1 gill cream for filling
Toasted flaked almonds or coconut for the sides of the cake.

Prepare the butter sponge in the usual way and bake the mixture for preference in a ring cake tin.

When cold, split and sandwich together with some of the coffee-flavoured butter icing. Spread this icing on the sides of the cake also and roll in the toasted nuts. Lastly, ice the top of the cake, roughing the butter icing into peaks.

The decoration is very easy, especially if the brandy snaps have been made in advance and are to hand in a tin. Arrange them like the spokes of a wheel around the top of the cake, allowing one to each slice. Pipe with whipped cream and serve as soon as possible.

MERINGUE LAYER CAKE

Thin layers of an almond meringue mixture and butter sponge are sandwiched together with a coffee-flavoured crème au beurre to form this luscious variation of a coffee cake.

FIG. 7. *Brandy Snap Cake.*
(I)—an exciting gateau for party catering. The decoration is easy,
providing the brandy snaps are to hand in a tin
(II)—slices easily to give an attractive portion

Almond meringue:
4 egg whites   4 oz flaked almonds
4 oz castor sugar

Butter sponge:
4 oz margarine   4 oz flour
4 oz castor sugar   1 small teaspoon baking powder
2 eggs

Coffee crème au beurre:
3 oz granulated sugar   8 oz butter
6 tablespoons water   coffee essence to flavour
3 yolks of egg

Begin by making the almond meringue:—cover three baking sheets with greaseproof paper and draw an 8–8¾ inch circle on each, using a cake tin as a guide. Grease.

Now whisk the egg whites until very stiff and gradually beat in half the sugar. Fold in the remainder, together with the flaked almonds. These should be chopped a little if very rough.

Divide between the three prepared tins and spread to give three circles almost a ¼ inch thick. Sprinkle one of these with more flaked almonds and dust all three with castor sugar. Bake, as for meringues, for approximately 1 hour in an oven set at ½, B–A or 300°.

Now prepare the butter sponge:—cream the margarine and sugar together until light. Gradually beat in the lightly-whisked eggs and, with the last of the egg, add the flour and baking powder. Bake this mixture in an 8–8¾ inch cake tin. The time required will be approximately 30 minutes and the oven should be set at 5, D or 400°.

Lastly prepare the crème au beurre:—put the sugar and water into a small saucepan and stir over a gentle heat until dissolved. Remove the spoon and bring to the boil. Boil gently until 216° is reached or until a little, when tested in cold water, will form a "thread" between the finger and thumb. Pour gently on to the egg yolks, beating all the time, and continue whisking until light and thick.

Cream the butter and gradually beat in the egg mixture. Flavour with coffee essence and use to sandwich the cake together as follows:—split the butter sponge in two and sandwich with the layers of almond meringue. These may need trimming a little. Use a circle of meringue as a base for the cake and reserve the layer which has been sprinkled with flaked almonds as the top. In this way no further decoration is necessary for this cake.

FLAVOURED WITH GINGER

GINGER may be used to flavour cakes in a variety of ways apart from the traditional gingerbread and a supply of ground ginger, ginger preserved in syrup and China ginger should be kept in every kitchen cupboard. They have many uses, for example, I like to use the syrup from a jar of ginger when making water icing or to add chopped ginger, instead of dried fruit, when baking little buns. If these are iced as suggested they are very tempting. Interesting afternoon tea scones may also be made using a combination of chopped walnuts and ginger; serve them hot and well-buttered if you wish for compliments!

SPONGY GINGERBREAD

Gingerbread is easy to mix but is not so easy to bake, since it will sink in the centre if disturbed in any way during the baking process. As it browns readily it is advisable to place it on the middle shelf of a moderately-heated oven; then leave it, without even opening the oven door, until it should be almost baked.

8 oz flour	*2 oz raisins*
½ teaspoon salt	*3 oz margarine*
½ teaspoon baking soda	*1 tablespoon syrup*
¼ teaspoon ground ginger	*1 tablespoon treacle*
¼ teaspoon ground cinnamon	*1 egg*
2 oz demerara sugar	*approx 1 gill buttermilk*
4 oz China ginger (chopped)	*½ oz flaked almonds to sprinkle on top*

Sieve the flour, salt, baking soda and spices together. Add the sugar, ginger and fruit. Meanwhile heat the margarine, syrup and treacle together in a saucepan until melted, but not hot. Stir in the well-beaten egg and some of the buttermilk and use to mix all to a thick pouring consistency. Pour into a flat baking tin (one 8 inch square is satisfactory) which has been lined with greased paper. Sprinkle the top with flaked almonds and bake in a moderately-heated oven for approximately ³⁄₄–1 hour (3, C or 375°).

A GINGER LOAF
to be served sliced and thickly-buttered

1 lb flour	3 oz margarine
¹⁄₂ teaspoon baking soda	5 oz golden syrup
1 teaspoon mixed spice	3 oz brown sugar
1 teaspoon ground ginger	2 eggs
4 oz currants	approx 1 gill buttermilk
4 oz China ginger	

Sieve the flour, baking soda and spices together. Add the fruit, chopped ginger and peel and mix thoroughly. Melt the margarine, syrup and sugar over a gentle heat. Stir in the 2 well-beaten eggs and use to mix all to a light batter which will pour easily. Use buttermilk as necessary to obtain this result. Pour into a prepared 2-lb loaf tin and bake in a moderate oven for approximately 1¹⁄₂ hours (2–3, C–B or 350°).

GRASMERE GINGERBREAD

The Lake District is renowned, not only for its beautiful scenery, but also for a particular variety of gingerbread known as Grasmere or Westmorland gingerbread. Its distinctive feature lies in the interesting combination of orange and lemon with the ginger flavour, giving a biscuit which is unique and delicious.

¹⁄₂ lb flour	1 teaspoon ground ginger
4 oz castor sugar	pinch salt
6 oz margarine	rind of ¹⁄₂ an orange
¹⁄₄ teaspoon baking soda	rind of ¹⁄₂ a lemon
¹⁄₄ teaspoon cream of tartar	1 tablespoon chopped preserved ginger if wished

Sieve the dry ingredients into a bowl, cut and rub in the margarine. Add the finely-chopped preserved ginger and the orange and lemon rind. At this stage the mixture should resemble cake crumbs. Press half the quantity firmly into a greased tin measuring 9 by 6 inches, and sprinkle the remainder evenly on top. Bake in a moderately-heated oven for approximately 1 hour. Serve cut in finger pieces.

PARKIN

The North of England, particularly the district around Leeds, is noted for a special form of gingerbread called Parkin. It is not unlike ordinary gingerbread except that oatmeal is included instead of a proportion of the flour. Well-made parkin is pleasantly moist to eat and is best when a few days, or even a week old. A popular pudding in the North consists of freshly-baked parkin smothered in stewed apples.

8 oz flour	*2 oz margarine*
2 teaspoons baking powder	*2 oz lard*
2 teaspoons ground ginger	*6 oz syrup*
8 oz oatmeal	*6 oz treacle*
4 oz castor sugar	*approx ½ cup milk*

Sieve the flour with the baking powder and the spice. Add the oatmeal and the sugar and cut and rub in the two fats. Heat the syrup and treacle slightly and stir in some of the milk. Use to mix all to a soft pouring consistency. Pour into a lined and greased swiss-roll tin and bake in a moderately-heated oven for ¾–1 hour. Serve cut into squares.

PRESERVED-GINGER CAKE

Preserved-ginger cake is quite different from the conventional gingerbread—it is light coloured, rich, generally coated with white icing and decorated with neat slices of ginger.

6 oz margarine	*¼ teaspoon ground ginger*
5 oz sugar	*a little grated lemon rind*
3 eggs	*6 oz preserved ginger*
8 oz flour	*1 tablespoon ginger syrup*
1 small teaspoon baking powder	

Icing:
    10 oz icing sugar   *boiling water*
    a little ginger syrup

Decoration:
    Slices of preserved ginger

Cream the margarine and sugar well and grate in a little lemon rind. Beat the eggs until light and gradually combine with the margarine and sugar. Lastly, stir in the ginger syrup, flour, baking powder, spice and chopped ginger. Turn into a prepared 2-lb cake tin and bake in a moderate oven for approximately 1-1¼ hours. When cold, spread with the water icing and decorate with slices of preserved ginger. Alternatively, chopped preserved ginger may be scattered over the top of the cake and water icing used to veil it. Again, a few whole cherries under the icing are attractive and show through in a most appetising way.

GINGER SHORTCAKE

Ginger shortcake is a most unusual and interesting cake. The basic mixture consists of three rounds of an almond shortcake; these are put together and iced with a particularly good form of ginger butter icing. Flaked toasted almonds and ginger are used for decoration. Remember, the finished cake must be put aside for a few days to mellow before cutting and in this time the biscuit mixture softens so that the cake is easy to cut and eat.

2 oz flour   *3 oz castor sugar*
2 oz rice flour   *½ teaspoon ground ginger*
4 oz margarine   *1 yolk of egg to hind*
3 oz ground almonds

Ginger icing:

3 oz margarine   *1 tablespoon cream*
4½ oz icing sugar   *a little ginger syrup and ground*
1 dessertspoon chopped almonds   *ginger to flavour*
2 dessertspoons finely chopped ginger

Decoration :

2 oz flaked almonds   a little green vermicelli
a few pieces of ginger

Put the flour and rice flour into a bowl and cut and rub in the margarine. Add the ground almonds, spice and sugar, and mix all to a stiff paste using yolk of egg. Divide into three portions and roll each out into a circle, rather more than a ¼-inch thick. Place in lined 6-inch sandwich tins, and bake in a moderate oven (5, D or 375°).

Make the butter icing in the usual way, beating in the finely chopped almonds and preserved ginger. Add the cream and flavour with ground ginger and ginger syrup. Use to sandwich the three rounds of biscuit together. Ice the sides and roll in the toasted shredded almonds. Finally cover the top of the cake with the butter icing. Rough up into points and decorate with almonds, pieces of ginger and green vermicelli.

A GINGER SPONGE SANDWICH

Sponge sandwich :

3 eggs   1 tablespoon lemon juice
5½ oz castor sugar   1½ oz preserved ginger
3½ oz flour   ¾ teaspoon baking powder
1 tablespoon water

Filling :

2 oz margarine   ½ teaspoon ground ginger
3 oz icing sugar

Icing :

10 oz icing sugar   boiling water
squeeze of lemon juice

Chop the ginger finely and toss in the sieved flour and baking powder.

Next separate the whites from the yolks of egg and beat the former until stiff. Then gradually beat in the yolks and the sugar, adding these alternately and whisking well between each addition. When the mixture is thick, fold in the flour mixture and the water and lemon juice. Divide between two prepared sandwich tins and bake in a moderate oven for approximately 25 minutes.

When cold, sandwich with the ginger-flavoured butter icing and ice the top and sides of the cake with white water icing. Decorate with neat slices of ginger.

A DARK GINGER CAKE

Richer than the usual gingerbread, this ginger cake makes a pleasant cutting cake.

4 oz margarine	*8 oz flour*
4 oz castor sugar	*½ teaspoon ground ginger*
2 eggs	*½ teaspoon baking powder*
1 dessertspoon syrup	*4 oz preserved ginger*
1 tablespoon treacle	*½ oz chopped walnut*

Cream the margarine and sugar thoroughly, then beat in the well-whisked eggs, the syrup and treacle. With the last of these add the flour, ground ginger, baking powder and chopped preserved ginger. Turn into a lined 7-inch cake tin. Sprinkle with chopped walnuts and bake in a moderate oven (4, C or 375°) for approximately 1¼ hours.

AN OLD-FASHIONED FLAVOURING

ADMITTEDLY, caraway seeds are not to everyone's liking and they might well be considered an old-fashioned flavouring. Certainly they are more likely to be appreciated by the older members of the family. Should you belong to a divided household and yet wish to use caraways occasionally in order to please some, then I suggest you use them in scones, bread or little buns. These are quickly made and eaten and are probably better than a rich seed cake which will remain for a long time to haunt the lives of that half of the family who cannot tolerate caraways at all.

CARAWAY BREAD

Caraway bread is delicious served fresh, spread generously with sweet butter, and accompanied by a really good cup of tea.

1/2 lb flour	3 oz margarine
1/2 teaspoon baking soda	1 oz castor sugar
1/2 teaspoon cream of tartar	1 dessertspoon caraway seeds
1/2 teaspoon salt	approx 1/4–1/2 pint milk

Sieve the flour, baking soda, cream of tartar and salt into a bowl. Cut and rub in the margarine. Add the sugar and caraway seeds and mix all to a soft dough with the milk. Turn the mixture into a greased 1 lb loaf tin and bake in a fairly hot oven for approximately 3/4 hour. Alternatively make into a round cake and mark into farls as in the making of soda bread.

CARAWAY BUNS

1/2 lb flour	4 oz castor sugar
1 teaspoon baking powder	3 teaspoons caraway seeds
1/2 teaspoon salt	1 egg
4 oz margarine	milk to mix

75

Sieve the flour, baking powder and salt into a bowl. Cut and rub in the margarine. Add the sugar and the caraway seeds. Beat the egg lightly and use to mix all to a very stiff dough. Divide out in small rough heaps on to a greased baking tray and bake in a hot oven for approximately 15 minutes. Serve while still very fresh.

ROUGH ROBIN CAKES

In these cakes the seeds are not so evident, and they may safely be offered to those who, in the ordinary way, are intolerant of caraways.

6 oz flour	*2 oz sugar*
2 oz ground rice	*½ teaspoon caraway seeds*
½ teaspoon salt	*3 oz sultanas*
1 teaspoon baking powder	*1 oz candied peel*
4 oz margarine	*milk to mix*

Sieve the flour, ground rice, salt and baking powder into a bowl. Cut and rub in the margarine. Add the sugar, caraway seeds, fruit and peel. Mix to a very stiff dough with the milk. Turn the mixture into a flat greased tin and spread so that it is about ¾-inch thick. A tin measuring 9 by 6 inches is very suitable. Bake in a hot oven for approximately 30 minutes. Dust with sugar and cut into fingers.

Serve while very fresh.

SEED CAKE

6 oz margarine	*8 oz flour*
6 oz sugar	*small ½ oz caraway seed*
3 eggs	*¼ teaspoon baking powder*

Cream the margarine and sugar until very soft. Whisk the eggs until frothy and gradually beat into the margarine and sugar mixture. With the last of the egg commence adding the flour. Beat the flour in lightly and with the last of the flour add the baking powder and caraway seeds. Turn the mixture into a prepared cake tin and bake in a moderate oven.

An old-fashioned flavouring

Note : This recipe may also be used to make an excellent sultana cake. The caraway seeds should be omitted and a $\frac{1}{4}$ lb sultanas added, together with 1 oz peel and a pinch of ground nutmeg and ground mace.

CARAWAY SHORTBREAD

The enthusiast for caraways will also enjoy shortbread which has been flavoured by rolling a few seeds into the mixture. Simply sprinkle a pinch over the biscuit dough during the rolling process and roll in lightly. Then bake the cake in the usual way and serve dusted with castor sugar.

CARAWAY AND LEMON BISCUITS

4 oz margarine
7 oz castor sugar
1 egg
12 oz flour
grated rind of 1 lemon

2 tablespoons lemon juice
$\frac{1}{2}$ teaspoon salt
$\frac{1}{4}$ teaspoon baking soda
2 teaspoons caraway seeds

Cream the margarine and sugar in the usual way and gradually beat in the lightly-whisked egg. Finally work in the other ingredients; the mixture should form a stiff dough. Turn out on to a floured board, roll out and cut into biscuits. Bake in a moderate oven set at 4–5, D or 375°, until golden and crisp.

MERINGUES AND MERINGUE CAKES

MERINGUES are always popular, while meringue mixture lends itself to a much greater variety of uses than many suppose. It is quick to make, too, so is invaluable to busy housewives.

MERINGUES

While meringues are not really difficult to make, some find the knack elusive. Perhaps the fault is that the whites are not really beaten stiffly enough, or perhaps the work of mixing and shaping is carried out too slowly; or again, it may be that the baking is at fault.

This recipe is the standard one and two or three whites make a useful quantity:

3 egg whites　　　　　　　　　　　　　　*6 oz castor sugar*
a pinch of salt

Add a pinch of salt to the egg whites and whisk until very stiff. The sugar is then added and this may be done in different ways depending on the type of meringue required and the circumstances:—

1. If a very light open-textured meringue is required then the castor sugar should be lightly folded into the whites of egg.

2. If, however, a closer-textured meringue is wanted, a proportion of the sugar should be beaten into the whisked whites. Once the whites are really stiff the sugar should be added, a spoonful at a time. Sprinkle it lightly over the whites and beat it in thoroughly. Any amount from a spoonful to the full quantity may be added in this way according to the discretion of the cook. The higher proportion of sugar beaten in, the closer the texture and the stiffer the meringue. Such meringue is particularly suitable for piping.

3. If an electric mixing machine is being used for whipping the whites for meringues, then it is convenient to continue using it when adding the sugar. Obviously this can easily be beaten in, but if an open-textured meringue is required proceed as follows:—

Whisk the whites until really stiff. Then beat in a teaspoonful of sugar to each white, adding each teaspoonful separately, beating well in between each addition. Now turn the speed of the machine back to slow and shoot in the remainder of the sugar from a piece of paper. Quickly turn the speed up to high and then switch off immediately. This should all be done in a matter of seconds. The meringue mixture is now ready for use.

To shape meringues:—it is most important, if the meringues are to hold their shape, that the folding-in of the sugar and the shaping should be done quickly. Any delay may cause the mixture to go soft, therefore have 2–3 baking sheets prepared and a cool oven in readiness before starting to make the meringues. The baking sheets should be very lightly greased and dusted with flour.

The simplest method of shaping the meringues is to use two spoons. Teaspoons, dessertspoons or tablespoons are all suitable according to the size required, but remember, when deciding, that the meringues are generally used in pairs, and also that the mixture will expand with the heat in the oven. Fill one spoon neatly with the meringue mixture and then scoop it out with the second spoon to form an oval meringue with a pleasant ridge down the centre.

Alternatively, put the mixture into a forcing bag fitted with a large star or plain pipe and force out in fancy shapes or "bulbs."

Always dredge meringues with sugar before placing in the oven. This ensures a dry surface.

Baking the meringues:—it is wise to bake meringues after the oven has been thoroughly heated for some other purpose. In an electric oven the thermometer should be at 300°. Using a gas oven there should be a low flame and the meringues should be placed on the lowest shelf. The advised regulo setting is ½ or B later reduced to A. Remember, too, it is possible to cook meringues too slowly. This fault can usually be recognised because they will ooze syrup, and are difficult to remove from the baking sheet.

Meringues will require 2–3 hours to bake according to size and often the heat can be turned off before the cooking is complete. This applies particularly when using a well insulated electric oven. When ready they should be an attractive golden colour and should store perfectly in an air-tight tin.

SOME PLEASANT VARIATIONS WITH MERINGUE SHELLS

Meringue shells are usually filled with vanilla-flavoured, sweetened, whipped cream. Served like this they are correctly spoken of as "meringues chantilly," which is a pretty name for a pretty dish.

When strawberries are in season these may be used with whipped cream as follows:—

When the meringue shells are almost cooked remove from the baking sheet and gently push in the soft centre. Return to the oven and dry out completely. When required for use, put a little whipped, sweetened cream in the cavity, then a strawberry whole or sliced and sandwich two together with cream in the usual way. The strawberries make a pleasant surprise inside.

In the autumn a chestnut preserved in vanilla-flavoured syrup might be used, or, alternatively, fill the cavity with chestnut purée which can be bought already prepared, sweetened and flavoured with vanilla. Sandwich two of these together with whipped cream.

COFFEE MERINGUES

Coffee meringues are an interesting variation of the foregoing recipe and should be served filled with coffee-flavoured whipped cream.

3 whites of egg	*1 teaspoon Nescafé*
6 oz castor sugar	*a good pinch of salt*

Add the salt to the whites of egg and whisk in a cool place until very stiff. Whisk in three pinches of sugar. Then combine the Nescafé with the remainder of the sugar and lightly and quickly fold into the whites. Shape the meringues by either piping out on to greased and floured baking trays, or alternatively shape by using two spoons. Dust with sugar and dry off in a cool oven. If desired the whipped cream used to fill coffee meringues may also be flavoured with coffee.

LEMON MERINGUE BASKETS

The combination of lemon and meringue is always good and unusual and fresh-flavoured little cakes may be made as follows:—

Prepare meringue from two whites of egg, beating in all the sugar so that the mixture is very stiff. Place in a forcing bag fitted with a $\frac{1}{4}$-inch plain pipe, and pipe out tiny meringue baskets on to a greased and floured tray. Make the base first by piping the mixture spiral fashion until it is about $1\frac{1}{2}$ inches across, then continue and pipe a spiral wall around the outer edge. Dust with sugar and dry off in a cool oven. Serve filled with lemon curd and topped with whipped cream if liked.

MERINGUES—MONT BLANC STYLE

A luscious combination of meringue, chestnut purée and whipped cream.

Meringue should be prepared in the usual way and the mixture piped out into "bulbs" using a plain éclair pipe. Bake as before and store until required in an air-tight tin.

When required have ready a chestnut purée prepared as follows:—

¾ lb chestnuts	3 oz sugar
a little milk	¾ gill water
vanilla essence	1½ oz butter

Make a slit in each chestnut and put in a pan with cold water to cover. Bring to the boil and simmer for a few minutes. Then remove from the water, a few at a time and peel off both the outer and inner skin.

Now stew the chestnuts in a little vanilla-flavoured milk and, when tender, drain and sieve.

Meanwhile put the sugar and water into a small saucepan and once the sugar has dissolved simmer until a heavy syrup has formed. Cool slightly.

Finally, beat the butter and syrup into the sieved chestnuts. The purée is now ready for making up the meringues—Mont Blanc style. One meringue shell is used as the base for each cake and on it is piped a bulb of whipped cream. Put the chestnut purée into an icing bag fitted with a coarse writing pipe and pipe backwards and forwards over the meringue and cream. Pipe generously with the purée so as to form an attractive dome. Dust with icing sugar and serve.

If preferred the chestnut purée may be purchased already prepared. It is sold in tubes or tins but, although convenient, it is expensive and not so plentiful.

PAVLOVA

One of the most attractive uses for meringue is in the making of a Pavlova. The name in itself is lovely and it is interesting to know that this dish was first made in New Zealand in honour of the great Russian dancer. The meringue mixture is shaped into the form of a cake and it is only baked long enough to give a crisp, golden crust but with the mixture still soft, like marshmallow, in the centre. When baked and cold it may be finished in a variety of ways. For example, different fruit may be used as convenient:—in New Zealand pineapple and passion fruit pulp are favoured, while in this country raspberries and strawberries are delicious and colourful. Tinned fruit is also good but in any case the fruit is finally covered with a generous layer of whipped cream and the whole sprinkled with toasted flaked almonds.

Lemon-cream Pavlova or chocolate Pavlova are also good and incidentally very practical, in that the yolks, available after making the meringue, are used in the filling.

The ingredients for the meringue mixture are as follows :—

3 whites of egg   6 oz castor sugar
a pinch of salt   1 small teaspoon vinegar

*Prepare the baking sheet first :—*line the bottom of a flat baking tray with greaseproof paper and, using a 7-inch cake tin as a guide, draw a circle. Grease. Then hold under the cold tap for a moment, and lastly shake off any surplus water.

*Now prepare the meringue :—*whisk the three whites of egg with a pinch of salt until they are really stiff. Add the sugar and the vinegar and carefully fold in. Turn on to the prepared paper and spread neatly to form a round cake about $1\frac{1}{2}$ inches thick. Dust the top and sides with castor sugar and bake in a slow oven for $1\frac{1}{4}$ hours. Exact baking instructions are as follows:—

Electric ovens—325° for $\frac{3}{4}$ hour, then switch off for the remaining $\frac{1}{2}$ hour.

Gas ovens—Regulo 1 or B for $\frac{3}{4}$ hour and then turn down to $\frac{1}{2}$ or A for the remainder of the time.

Note. These temperatures are a little higher than those normally recommended for meringues.

When the mixture is cooked, turn over and remove the paper; it should come away quite easily. Place on a serving dish and finish in one of the following ways:—

LEMON CREAM PAVLOVA. While the meringue is in the oven prepare a lemon cream filling:—

3 yolks of egg   the rind and juice of 1 lemon
3 oz sugar

Beat the yolks and the sugar together until creamy and light. Add the lemon rind

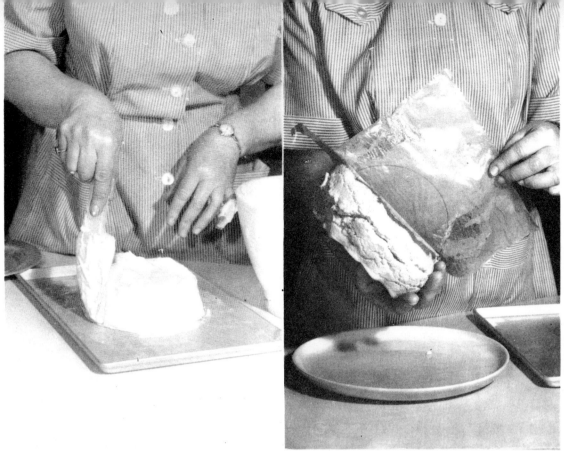

FIG. 8. *Pavlova.*
(I) Spread the meringue neatly to form a round cake.
(II) When the meringue is cooked, turn over and remove the paper—it should
come away quite easily.
(III) One of the most attractive uses for meringue

juice and transfer all to a small saucepan. Cook gently until the mixture thickens. Cool a little, then spread this lemon mixture on top of the Pavlova and cover thickly with whipped cream. Sprinkle with toasted flaked almonds and decorate round the edge with 5 or 6 whole cherries.

PINEAPPLE PAVLOVA. Open a tin of pineapple and strain off the juice. Reserve a portion of the fruit for decoration and chop the remainder. Spread the chopped pineapple over the Pavlova. Cover thickly with whipped cream and decorate with pieces of pineapple and toasted flaked almonds.

STRAWBERRY PAVLOVA. A strawberry Pavlova is made in a similar manner to the pineapple Pavlova; the greater part of a punnet of strawberries should be sliced, dusted with castor sugar, and then spread on the meringue. Cover generously with whipped cream and decorate with whole strawberries.

CHOCOLATE PAVLOVA

The recipe for this version of a Pavlova is slightly different. The ground cinnamon included in the meringue and in the whipped cream is novel and very good.

Meringue mixture:

4 whites of egg	1 teaspoon vinegar
a pinch of salt	$\frac{1}{2}$ teaspoon ground cinnamon
8 oz castor sugar	

Chocolate mixture:

4 yolks of egg	$\frac{1}{2}$ cup water
6 oz dark chocolate	

Cream mixture:

1 gill cream	$\frac{1}{4}$ teaspoon ground cinnamon
$1\frac{1}{2}$ tablespoons castor sugar	

Make the Pavlova cake as already described adding the ground cinnamon with the sugar.

While it is baking make the chocolate filling:—melt the chocolate over hot water. Then stir in the water and the 4 yolks of egg. Cook gently until it thickens and use to spread over the top of the Pavlova. Cover with the cinnamon-flavoured, whipped cream and decorate with a sprinkling of coarsely-grated chocolate.

PEACH VACHERIN

Another lovely dish—half cake, half sweet—serve it as it suits you best.

Peach Vacherin consists of three layers of meringue sandwiched with sliced peaches and whipped cream. The meringue should be piped, two rounds in the form of a spiral and one round, to form the top layer, in the form of a trellis, which shows off the filling prettily.

For the meringue you will require :—

3 whites of egg	*6 oz castor sugar*
a pinch of salt	

and for the filling 1 tin sliced peaches and whipped cream

Prepare three baking trays first, line them with greaseproof paper and on each draw a circle round a sandwich tin. Grease.

Next prepare the meringue :—whisk the whites of egg with a pinch of salt until very stiff. Gradually beat in the castor sugar. Transfer to a forcing bag fitted with a rose pipe. Pipe out to give three circles, two in the form a spiral and one trellised and finished round the edge with stars. Be careful to keep all three the same size—the top one tends to spread. Decorate the trellised layer still further with quarters of cherry arranged at intervals on the border of stars and sprinkle in between with flaked almonds. Dust all three layers with sugar before baking in a very moderate oven as for ordinary meringues. Suggested oven temperature—$\frac{1}{4}$, A or 300° reduced to 200°.

When required put together with the fruit and cream. The peaches should, of course, be drained free of juice and it is attractive if they show at the edges.

A STRAWBERRY MERINGUE CAKE

Strawberry meringue cake is equally at home on the tea-table or as a luscious pudding for a special occasion. It is unusual in that a thin layer of cake mixture is baked with a covering of meringue and you might well imagine that this arrangement would not really be feasible. In fact it works very well, the result having a good eating quality,

FIG. 9. *Peach Vacherin.*
(I) The meringue is piped—two rounds in the form of a spiral, and one round, to form the
top layer, in the form of a trellis
(II)—consists of three layers of meringue sandwiched with sliced peaches and whipped cream

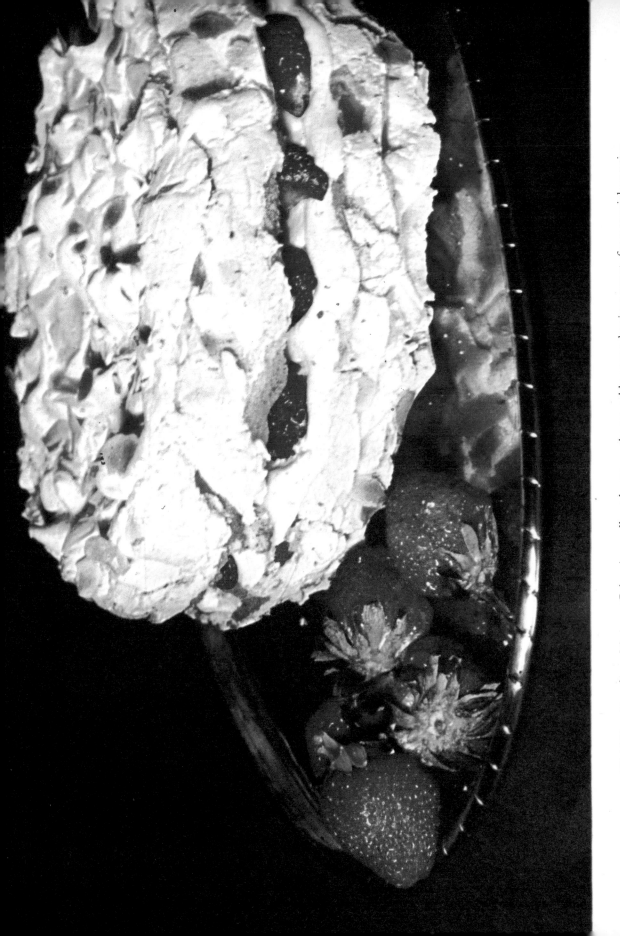

PLATE 2. *Strawberry Meringue Cake*—is equally at home on the tea-table or as a luscious sweet for a special occasion

FIG. 10. *Strawberry Meringue Cake.*
A thin layer of cake mixture is baked with a covering of meringue and two of these are
sandwiched together with a generous mixture of strawberries and whipped cream

as well as looking most attractive in the cross-section. Two of these are sandwiched
together with a generous mixture of strawberries and whipped cream and, while any
fruit might be used, one with a sharp flavour is best.

The cake mixture:

2 oz margarine	*a little vanilla essence*
4 oz castor sugar	*1 teaspoon baking powder*
4 yolks of egg	*5 tablespoons creamy milk*
4 oz flour	

Meringues and meringue cakes

The meringue :

4 *whites of egg* 2 *tablespoons flaked almonds*
8 *oz sugar*

The filling :

1 *punnet of strawberries (or packet of frozen ones)*
1 *cup cream* *sugar as necessary*

Line the bottom of two 9-inch cake tins with circles of greased paper.

Now prepare the cake mixture :—cream the margarine and the sugar together and, when light, beat in the yolks of egg adding these one at a time. Then add the flour and other ingredients alternately with the milk. Divide this mixture between the two tins and spread evenly.

Now make up the meringue :—add a pinch of salt to the whites of egg and whisk until stiff. Gradually beat in the sugar. Divide between the two cake tins and swirl attractively. Sprinkle one cake with the flaked almonds. Bake in a moderate oven for approximately 45 minutes. Suggested temperatures being 2, B or 350°.

When cold, sandwich generously with a mixture of fruit and whipped cream. The cake sprinkled with the almonds should be uppermost.

A CHAPTER ON BISCUITS

CRISP, freshly-made biscuits are something which everyone enjoys. They are, as a rule, easy to make but at the same time there are a few details, which, if observed, will give your work a more professional finish. In the first place, as far as the actual mixing is concerned, it is not necessary to put a great deal of energy into the creaming process. Biscuits are not like cakes in this respect and it is only necessary to soften the fat and sugar sufficiently to enable them to absorb the dry ingredients with ease. When rolling the biscuits it is important that each one should be of a uniform thickness. This is not merely on the score of neatness but, more important, because an occasional biscuit which is thinner will brown more quickly during the baking. Lastly the baking should be a slow process, in order to develop the nutty flavour associated with a good biscuit.

FLAKEMEAL BISCUITS

4 oz margarine	5 oz flakemeal or porridge oats
2 oz sugar	1/2 teaspoon salt
2 oz flour	a pinch of baking soda

Cream the margarine and sugar together and gradually work in the other ingredients. Turn on to a floured board sprinkled with flakemeal and roll out. Score with a fork to roughen the surface attractively, and cut into biscuits. Bake in a moderate oven set at 3, D or 375° until a light golden colour.

FLAKEMEAL AND ALMOND BISCUITS

A good variation of the above recipe is to add 2 oz chopped almonds to the mixture before rolling it out.

FLAKEMEAL SHORTBREAD

Busy housewives will appreciate the following recipe for its good eating qualities and speed of production.

4 oz margarine
2 oz demerara sugar
4 oz flakemeal or porridge oats

2½ oz flour
¼ teaspoon baking soda
a pinch of salt

Melt the margarine in a saucepan and stir in the remainder of the ingredients. Spread in a greased tin measuring approximately 6 by 9 inches. Press firmly with the blade of a knife, otherwise the biscuits are apt to be crumbly when cut. Bake slowly in a moderately-heated oven set at 3, C or 375° for about ¾ hour. Cut into fingers while hot.

COFFEE FLAKEMEAL BISCUITS

An iced biscuit has a special attraction and in the following recipe the combination of flakemeal, coconut, and coffee is very good indeed. The biscuits are sandwiched together with coffee butter icing and finished with coffee-flavoured water icing. An important feature is, that in spite of the filling and icing, these biscuits remain crisp if stored in an airtight tin.

4 oz margarine
2 oz castor sugar
1 dessertspoon golden syrup
5 oz flakemeal or porridge oats

2 oz flour
½ oz coconut
a pinch of baking soda
a pinch of salt

Filling:

1½ oz margarine
3 oz icing sugar

coffee essence

Icing:

4 oz icing sugar
coffee essence

boiling water

Decoration: half walnuts

Cream the margarine and sugar. Then beat in the syrup and gradually work in the dry ingredients. Turn on to a floured board and roll out fairly thickly. Cut into small rounds with a plain cutter and bake in a moderate oven set at 3, C or 375° until golden.

When cold prepare the filling :—cream the margarine and gradually beat in the sieved icing sugar. Beat until light and then flavour with coffee essence. Use to sandwich two biscuits together.

Next prepare the icing :—sieve the icing sugar, add some coffee essence and mix to a spreading consistency with boiling water. Using a teaspoon, put a little on top of each biscuit. Decorate the centre with a half walnut.

ORANGE CREAM BISCUITS

The nature of these biscuits is such that the mixture spreads while in the oven into a smiling, crinkly biscuit, which is later sandwiched with another using an orange filling. If preferred, the orange flavouring may be omitted and the biscuit put together with melted chocolate instead. This version is called a Gipsy Cream.

4 oz margarine	$\frac{1}{2}$ *teaspoon salt*
4 oz castor sugar	$\frac{1}{2}$ *teaspoon cream of tartar*
1 dessertspoon golden syrup	$\frac{1}{2}$ *teaspoon baking soda*
rind of 1 orange	*1 yolk of egg*
7 oz flour	

Filling :

$1\frac{1}{2}$ *oz margarine*	*a little grated orange rind*
3 oz icing sugar	*peach colouring*

Cream the margarine and sugar together and beat in the syrup and the orange rind. Gradually work in the sieved dry ingredients. Form the mixture into small balls and place well apart on a greased baking tray. Bake in a moderate oven set at 3, C or 375° for about 25 minutes or until golden in colour.

When cold prepare the filling :—cream the margarine and gradually work in the other ingredients. Use to sandwich two biscuits together.

This quantity should make approximately 18 biscuits.

ORANGE PRINCESS BISCUITS

Orange Princess biscuits are piped into finger shapes and when baked they are glazed, first with hot apricot jam, and then with orange water icing. This is done while they are hot and they are then returned to the oven for another minute or two. The icing sets attractively and the biscuits will retain their crispness. This is largely on account of the apricot jam under the icing; it appears to act like a waterproof coating and prevent the moistness of the icing penetrating.

The glaze and the icing are easy to apply, incidentally, since both can be painted on with a pastry brush. If wished, the ends of the biscuits may be dipped in melted chocolate.

4 oz margarine	*4 oz flour*
1 oz icing sugar	*rind of 1 orange*

Glaze:

approximately 2 tablespoons hot apricot jam

Icing:

3 oz icing sugar	*boiled juice of 1 orange*

Cream the margarine and sugar until very soft. This is important otherwise the mixture is too stiff to pipe with ease. Gradually work in the grated orange rind and the flour. Put into a forcing bag fitted with a large star pipe and pipe into finger shapes. Put aside in a cool place for about an hour. Then bake until golden in an oven set at 3, C or 375°.

Meanwhile heat the apricot jam and make the orange icing. When the biscuits are golden brown remove from the oven and brush with the apricot jam. Then brush the orange icing on top and return all to the oven for about one minute to set the icing.

When cold trim away any untidiness and dip the ends of the biscuits in melted chocolate and then in chocolate vermicelli.

SHAH BISCUITS

4 oz margarine
4 oz castor sugar
1 dessertspoon golden syrup
1 yolk of egg
7 oz flour
½ teaspoon cream of tartar

½ teaspoon baking soda
1 teaspoon ground ginger
a pinch of mixed spice
a pinch of ground cloves
a pinch of salt

Cream the margarine and sugar and beat in the syrup. Add the yolk of egg and gradually work in the sieved dry ingredients. Using floured hands, shape into small balls and place well apart on greased trays. Bake in an oven set at 3, C or 375° for approximately 20 minutes.

GINGER BISCUITS
suitable for gingerbread men and Christmas tree cookies

8 oz flour
4½ oz margarine
4 oz soft brown sugar

1 teaspoon ground ginger
2 oz treacle
2 oz golden syrup

Combine all the ingredients in a bowl and knead together until evenly coloured. Roll out on a floured board, cut into biscuits as required and bake in a moderate oven at 3, C or 375° approximately 20 minutes.

ALMOND MACAROONS

1–1½ whites of egg
4 oz castor sugar
2 oz almonds

½ oz ground almonds
1 teaspoon rice flour
a little almond essence

Blanch and chop the almonds finely. Combine with the other dry ingredients. Half whip the white of egg and fold in the other ingredients. The consistency should be fairly stiff. Put out with a teaspoon on to a tray lined with rice paper. Decorate with a sprinkling of flaked almonds and a piece of cherry. Bake at 3, B or 325° for approximately 40 minutes.

WALNUT MACAROONS

Those who enjoy nuts will like these biscuits. They are somewhat similar to almond macaroons, but when baked, are sandwiched together with coffee butter icing.

$1\frac{1}{2}$ *whites of egg*	*4 oz castor sugar*
2 oz finely chopped walnuts	*1 teaspoon rice flour*
$\frac{1}{2}$ *oz ground almonds*	

Filling:

$1\frac{1}{2}$ *oz margarine*	*coffee essence to flavour*
3 oz icing sugar	*a few quarter walnuts to decorate*

Half whisk the whites of egg and fold in the other ingredients. Put out in small teaspoonfuls on to a baking tin lined with rice paper. Decorate every second biscuit with a piece of walnut. Bake at 3, "B" or 325° for approximately 40 minutes.

When cold, sandwich two together with the coffee butter icing.

Note: These are perhaps even better made with chopped Brazil nuts.

ALMOND FINGERS

Pastry:

5 oz flour	*2 yolks of egg*
a pinch of salt	*a little water if necessary*
3 oz margarine	*apricot or raspberry jam*

Almond mixture:

2 whites of egg	*3 oz ground almonds*
6 oz castor sugar	*almond essence*
1 oz flaked almonds to sprinkle over the top	

Prepare the pastry first:—sieve the flour and salt and cut and rub in the margarine. Mix to a stiff paste with the yolks of egg and a little water.

Divide the pastry into two or three portions and roll each into a strip about 3–3½ inches wide and the length of a baking tray. Arrange on the tray and then cut a narrow strip from each of the long sides. Damp and turn over on to the larger piece of pastry to form an edging. Spread the centre with a little jam.

Next prepare the almond mixture :—half whisk the whites of egg and then fold in the sugar, ground almonds and the almond essence. Spread on top of the jam. Sprinkle with the flaked almonds and bake in a moderate oven 3, D or 375° for approximately 40 minutes. Cut into fingers.

COCONUT NIBBED FINGERS

Coconut nibbed fingers are similar to almond fingers in many ways and, while cheaper, are possibly equally good to eat.

Pastry :

5 oz flour	2 yolks of egg
a pinch of salt	a little water if necessary
3 oz margarine	
apricot jam	

Coconut filling :

2 whites of egg	1 teaspoon ground rice
6 oz castor sugar	a little vanilla essence
2½ oz coconut	1 oz flaked almonds to sprinkle over the top

Sieve the flour and salt and cut and rub in the margarine. Then mix all to a stiff dough using the yolks diluted with a little cold water. Roll out and use to line a rectangular baking sheet. Spread lightly with the apricot jam.

Next prepare the filling :—Whip the whites of egg lightly and fold in the sugar, coconut, ground rice and vanilla essence. Spread over the jam and sprinkle with the flaked almonds. Bake in a moderate oven at 3, D or 375° for approximately 40 minutes. Cut into fingers.

MASSERINES

Masserines are also similar to almond fingers in many respects, with the one great difference that the almond mixture is boiled before pouring into the pastry strips. This changes its character considerably and, if well made, the result should be glossy and crisp so that it breaks attractively on being cut into fingers.

Pastry:

5 oz flour	*1 oz castor sugar*
a pinch of salt	*1 yolk*
3 oz margarine	*a little water if necessary*

apricot or raspberry jam

Almond mixture:

1 white of egg	*2 oz flaked or shredded almonds*
3 oz castor sugar	*1 teaspoon cocoa*

Prepare the pastry strips:—cream the margarine and sugar and beat in the yolk of egg. Then gradually work in the flour and salt. A little water may be necessary if the mixture is too stiff. Divide into two or three portions and roll each into a long strip of about 3–4 inches wide. Arrange on a baking tray and cut a narrow strip from each of the long sides. Damp and turn over on to the larger piece of pastry to form an edging.

Spread the centre with jam.

Next prepare the almond mixture:—beat the white of egg until very stiff and fold in the sugar, cocoa and shredded almonds. Turn into a small saucepan and carefully heat until boiling. The mixture should be stirred all the time. Then spread quickly and evenly over the pastry. Bake in a moderate oven at 3, C or 350° for ¾–1 hour. Cut into fingers.

COFFEE BISCUITS

6 oz margarine	*6 oz flour*
1½ oz icing sugar	*Nescafé to flavour*

Filling:

either melted chocolate or coffee-flavoured butter icing

Cream the margarine and sugar until very soft. Then beat in the flavouring and the flour. The mixture is piped out into biscuits using either a narrow éclair or star pipe. Stand in a cool place for approximately 1 hour, then bake in a moderate oven at 3, C or 375°. When cold, sandwich two together with melted chocolate or coffee-flavoured butter icing.

WALNUT BISCUITS

2½ oz margarine	*¼ teaspoon baking soda*
2½ oz castor sugar	*¼ teaspoon cream of tartar*
4 oz flour	*a few half walnuts to decorate*

Filling: melted chocolate

Cream the margarine and sugar and gradually work in the dry ingredients. Form into small balls, hardly as big as a walnut. Flatten out on a greased tray and press a half walnut on every second biscuit. Bake in a moderate oven at 3, C or 375°. When cold, sandwich two together with melted chocolate.

VANILLA BISCUITS

4 oz margarine	*¼ teaspoon baking powder*
3 oz sugar	*¼ teaspoon vanilla essence*
2 oz flakemeal	*1 teaspoon golden syrup*
4 oz self-raising flour	*3 teaspoons boiling water*

Cream the margarine and sugar and gradually work in the other ingredients. Using floured hands shape into small balls. Flatten a little and arrange on a greased tray. Bake at 3, C or 375° until golden and crisp.

VANILLA COOKIES

4 oz margarine	*4½ oz flour*
3 oz castor sugar	*½ teaspoon baking powder*

1 teaspoon vanilla essence *a few split almonds or half-cherries*
to decorate

Melt the margarine in a saucepan and heat sufficiently to brown slightly. Then turn into a bowl and place over cold water to cool. Add the sugar and cream until light. Beat in the vanilla essence and gradually work in the flour and baking powder. Then, using floured hands, shape into small balls and flatten slightly. Place a split almond or a half-cherry on top of each biscuit and bake at 3, C or 375° until golden and crisp.

PEANUT BISCUITS
specially for those who enjoy peanuts

4 oz margarine *½ cup flour*
4 oz sugar *½ teaspoon baking powder*
1 egg *a pinch baking soda*
1 cup peanuts *a pinch salt*
1 cup flakemeal

Cream the margarine and sugar and gradually beat in the lightly-whisked egg, the roughly chopped nuts and the dry ingredients. Put out in small spoonfuls on a greased tray. Flatten with a fork, making a criss-cross mark and bake at 3, C or 375° for approximately 20–30 minutes.

A RICH OATCAKE

½ lb fine oatmeal *½ teaspoon baking soda*
1½ oz flour *¼ teaspoon cream of tartar*
1–2 oz sugar *½ teaspoon salt*
3 oz margarine *2 tablespoons milk*

Mix the dry ingredients and cut and rub in the margarine. Mix to a stiff dough using the milk. Roll out on a board sprinkled with oatmeal and cut into large biscuits. Bake in a moderate oven at 3, C or 375° for approximately 20 minutes.

Serve with and marmalade or honey.

Talking about cakes

ALMOND TUILES

When a dainty, crisp biscuit is required for serving with a cold sweet then Almond Tuiles are a good choice. The recipe is a French one, as you might guess, and the biscuits are interesting to make and look pretty when piled on a plate.

2 whites of egg	*½ teaspoon vanilla essence*
4 oz castor sugar	*2 oz flaked almonds*
2 oz flour	*2 oz melted margarine*

Whisk the whites of egg until stiff. Beat in the sugar and fold in the other ingredients.

The shaping is unusual and an important stage in the making of these biscuits. Put the mixture out in teaspoonfuls on to a greased tray. Allow only two to each baking sheet, and spread wafer-thin tising two forks. A small hole here and there is of no consequence. Bake in a moderate oven at 3, C or 375° until a delicate golden colour. Lift the biscuit off carefully and cool over a rolling pin. This gives each lacy biscuit a pretty and characteristic curl.

DUTCH FANS

Dutch Fans are dainty biscuits of unusual shape and are suitable to serve as a crisp accompaniment to many cold sweets.

9 oz flour	*2¼ oz castor sugar*
6¾ oz margarine	*½ an egg white*

Rub the fat into the flour. Add the sugar and bind to a stiff dough with the white of egg. Roll out thinly and cut into large circles with a fluted flan ring. Cut each circle into four fan shapes and bake in a moderate oven at 3, C or 375° until a delicate golden colour. Dust with castor sugar

CHECKERBOARD BISCUITS

A recipe for the neat-fingered who are prepared to take a little trouble in making something unusual. You will find them fascinating to make.

FIG. 11. *Almond Tuiles.*
(I) Pull the mixture wafer thin, using two forks. A small hole here
and there is of no consequence
(II) A dainty crisp biscuit suitable to serve with cold sweets

A batch each of plain and chocolate-coloured shortbread is required as follows:—

Plain shortbread:

6 oz flour	2 oz castor sugar
4 oz margarine	

Chocolate shortbread:

4 oz flour	2 oz castor sugar
2½ oz margarine	vanilla essence
2 teaspoons chocolate powder	a little egg yolk to bind

Make up both groups of ingredients as for shortbread.

Then proceed as follows:—

1. Cut the piece of plain shortbread into pieces of roughly two-thirds and one-third. Take the larger piece and roll into an oblong strip a ¼-inch thick.

2. Roll the chocolate-coloured shortcake into another strip ¼-inch thick.

3. Cut each of these strips into 3-inch widths.

4. Sandwich a chocolate and a plain strip together using a little egg white to stick them together.

5. Cut this three-inch strip in two and sandwich together again to give 1½-inch width of white, chocolate, white and chocolate. If the paste is too soft to handle with ease place in the refrigerator for a while to allow the block to set.

6. Now cut the block in four by the length and lay the pieces flat on the pastry board. Reverse the first and third strip and sandwich together again so as to give the checkerboard appearance.

7. Now roll out the remainder of the white shortbread and use to cover the checkerboard block, rather after the style of applying the marzipan to a Russian cake. Place in the refrigerator to harden.

8. Slice into individual biscuits each about ¼-inch thick.

9. Bake in a moderate oven at 3, C or 375° until golden and crisp.

NAPOLEON CAKES
toothsome, but for immediate use only

4 oz flour	1 oz castor sugar
3 oz margarine	1 egg yolk
1 oz ground almonds	raspberry jam

Rub the margarine into the flour and add the ground almonds and castor sugar. Then mix to a stiff paste with the yolk of egg. Turn on to a floured board and roll into a rectangular shape to fit a swiss-roll tin. Bake in a moderate oven until a delicate golden brown. Cut the piece of biscuit in two and spread one half with raspberry jam. Lift the other half on top and cut into fingers. Dust thickly with icing sugar.

EASTER BISCUITS

5 oz margarine
4 oz castor sugar
grated rind of 1 lemon
2 egg yolks

½ lb flour
a pinch of salt
2 oz currants

egg white and castor sugar to finish the top of the biscuits

Cream the margarine, sugar and lemon rind together. Then beat in the yolks and lastly work in the flour, salt and currants. The mixture should be stiff but if necessary leave it in a cool place for an hour or so to firm.

Turn the dough on to a board sprinkled with rice flour and roll out fairly thinly; cut into biscuits and brush with lightly-beaten white of egg. Sprinkle with sugar and bake in a moderate oven until a light golden colour. Suggested oven temperatures being 3, C or 375°.

DREAMING BREAD

SCOTLAND is justly famous for its shortbread but not many realise that in some remote parts of that country it serves as bride's cake. Indeed the story goes that, in days gone by, the cake of decorated shortbread was broken over the head of the bride as she entered her new home and the fragments given to her friends to dream on.

Good shortbread should always be made with butter in preference to margarine, since this gives it a beautiful flavour. Country butter is, I think, even better than creamery for this purpose, because of its more pronounced flavour.

Shortbread should be baked very slowly and given plenty of time. This slow baking imparts a special flavour which can be obtained in no other way. Conventionally too, shortbread is generally made in the form of a large thick cake, often marked into wedge shaped pieces. This is a very convenient and labour-saving method, although biscuits are sometimes preferred and are certainly quicker to bake.

SHORTBREAD

6 oz flour	*a pinch of baking powder*
1½ oz rice flour or ground rice	*a pinch of salt*
2 oz castor sugar	*5 oz butter*

Sieve the dry ingredients into a bowl. Add the butter and gradually knead all into a firm dough. Turn on to a floured board and roll into a round cake about ½ inch thick. Either place in a sandwich tin, or fasten a double band of greaseproof paper round the edge. Cut into triangles, prick and bake in a slow oven for approximately one hour. Dust with castor sugar. The actual temperature required for baking shortbread will vary according to the thickness of the cake—thick shortbread will require an oven temperature of approximately 2, B or 350°; shortbread biscuits 3, C or 375°.

Dreaming bread

ALMOND SHORTBREAD

The addition of chopped almonds to shortbread is very good. In some cases they are incorporated through the mixture, and in others they are rolled into the top of the cake as it is being shaped.

2 oz almonds	$\frac{1}{4}$ teaspoon baking powder
1 oz rice flour or ground rice	a pinch of salt
5 oz flour	4 oz butter

Blanch and chop the almonds. Sieve the dry ingredients into a basin, add the almonds and rub in the butter, gradually working all into a stiff dough. Turn on to a floured board and roll into a cake about $\frac{1}{2}$-inch thick. Place in a sandwich tin. Mark into triangles and bake slowly in a moderate oven. Sprinkle with castor sugar before turning out of the tin.

WALNUT SHORTBREAD
the addition of walnuts to shortbread is also good

$\frac{1}{2}$ lb flour	$1\frac{1}{2}$ oz chopped walnuts
2 oz cornflour	a little vanilla essence
3 oz castor sugar	$\frac{1}{2}$ lb butter

Place the dry ingredients in a bowl. Add the vanilla essence and the butter. Cut the latter into rough pieces, then crumb with the fingers and gradually work all into one piece. Towards the end of this process add the chopped walnuts.

Finally turn the mixture on to a floured board and shape as required; this quantity will give three cakes of shortbread using small round sandwich tins. Cut into triangular pieces, prick and bake in a moderate oven. Dust with castor sugar while still hot and in the tin.

COCONUT SHORTBREAD

$\frac{1}{2}$ lb flour	2 oz cornflour
4 oz castor sugar	a little vanilla essence
2 oz coconut	$\frac{1}{2}$ lb butter

Work the butter into the other ingredients until it forms a stiff dough. Turn the mixture on to a floured board and divide into three pieces. Roll each to fit a round sandwich tin. Cut into triangular wedges, prick and bake in a moderate oven at 3, C or 375° until golden and crisp. Dust with castor sugar before turning out of the tin.

PITCAITHLEY BANNOCK

Citron peel and almonds added to shortbread give the characteristic flavour and texture associated with a Pitcaithley bannock.

1 oz almonds	*3 oz rice flour or ground rice*
1 oz citron peel	*3 oz sugar*
6 oz flour	*4 oz butter*

Blanch and chop the almonds very finely, along with the 1 oz of citron peel. Add to the two flours. Work the butter and sugar together and gradually work in the dry ingredients. Turn on to a floured board and form into a round cake. Pinch the edges and lay on a baking sheet. Cut into triangular wedges and fasten a double strip of grease-proof paper around. Bake in a moderate oven for about 60 minutes.

SMALL CAKES IN VARIETY

THE variety of small cakes is immense and they form an essential item on the tea-table and for many party occasions. Often they are both rich and sweet, in which case it is essential to make them dainty and diminutive in size, otherwise they lose much of their attractiveness.

The following collection will be found to contain many of the cosy little recipes, so beloved by housewives in addition to the traditional favourites.

ALMOND CHEESE CAKES NO. 1

4 oz rich short crust or flaky pastry
a little apricot or raspberry jam

Filling:

2 whites of egg   *2 oz castor sugar*
2 oz ground almonds   *almond essence*

Use the pastry to line approximately 18 patty tins. Then put a little jam in the bottom of each.

Next prepare the almond filling:—lightly whisk the whites of egg and fold in the ground almonds, sugar and almond essence. Divide this mixture around the prepared tins. If wished the almond cheese cakes may be further decorated with a pastry cross or a sprinkling of flaked almonds. Bake in a moderate oven for approximately 20 minutes (5, D or 400°).

ALMOND CHEESE CAKES NO. 2

A more economical recipe, but still giving little cakes which are good to eat.

4 oz rich short crust or flaky pastry
a little apricot or raspberry jam

Filling:

1 white of egg
1½ oz ground almonds
3 oz castor sugar
1 teaspoon semolina

a little almond essence
a pinch each of baking soda and
    cream of tartar

Use the pastry to line approximately 2 dozen patty tins. Then put a little jam in each.

Now prepare the filling:—lightly whisk the white of egg and fold in the remainder of the ingredients. Divide around the prepared patty tins and bake in a moderate oven for approximately 20 minutes (5, D or 400°).

BRANDY SNAPS

Some people find brandy snaps difficult to make, but I feel the secret lies in the accurate measurement of the ingredients, care in not letting the mixture get more than warm when melting the ingredients, and in good organisation during the baking process. The cook should just be kept pleasantly busy with the brandy snaps as they come from the oven. They must be rolled fairly quickly and so, as a rule, it is better not to have more than two on a baking sheet at once, otherwise the wafer will have hardened before it is shaped. Should this happen, however, the fault may sometimes be corrected by returning it to the oven for a moment to soften again.

4 oz margarine
4 oz castor sugar
4 oz golden syrup

juice of ½ lemon
4 oz flour
1 small teaspoon ground ginger

whipped cream to fill

Put the margarine, sugar and syrup in a small saucepan and place over a gentle heat to melt. The mixture should on no account get hot, otherwise the flour, when added, will cook and prevent the mixture spreading in the oven. When melted stir in the lemon juice, flour and ground ginger. The mixture may be used immediately though some cooks prefer to chill it in a refrigerator before proceeding.

The baking process is best organised as follows:—if possible work with 3 or 4 greased baking sheets, according to the number of shelves in the oven. Ideally there should be one tray for each shelf and one in hand.

Put the mixture out in small teaspoonfuls, allowing two to each baking sheet and taking care to have them of an even size. Bake in a moderate oven to a rich brown. Then remove and allow to stand for a moment to cool slightly. Lift from the tray using a sharp pliable knife and quickly roll up, either round a greased horn mould or the greased handle of a wooden spoon.

Store in an airtight tin until required; then serve filled with whipped cream.

BRAZIL NUT KISSES

4 oz Brazil nuts   *1 white of egg*
2 oz hazel nuts   *6 oz demerara sugar*

First chop the nuts roughly. Then whisk the white of egg and fold in the sugar and nuts. Put the mixture out in small mounds on to trays lined with rice paper. As the little cakes are shaped press the ingredients together. They will be found to have little cohesion, so be patient, this is only to be expected. Finally bake in a moderate oven. They are soft when cooked, but will rapidly become crisp as they cool. The time depends on the size.

Sometimes Brazil Nut Kisses are decorated before baking, with a piece of cherry or a few pine kernels.

BROWN CAKES
spicy and good

6 oz flour   *½ teaspoon baking soda*
3 oz sultanas   *2 oz treacle*
3 oz castor sugar   *2 oz margarine*
a little grated nutmeg   *1 egg*
¾ teaspoon ground cinnamon

Mix the dry ingredients together in a bowl. Next, melt the treacle and margarine in a small saucepan. Stir in the beaten egg and use to mix all to a fairly soft batter. Divide around greased patty tins and bake in a fairly hot oven for 15–20 minutes (6, E or 425°).

BROWNIES
an American favourite

If the quantities in the recipe seem a little strange it is only because they have been converted from cups to ounces to make it easier for readers. The relatively large amount of sugar gives the brownies their characteristic and pleasant crust.

3½ oz margarine	3 oz flour
7 oz castor sugar	½ teaspoon baking powder
2 eggs	¼ teaspoon salt
½ teaspoon vanilla essence	4 oz chopped walnuts
2 oz dark chocolate	

Cream the margarine and sugar and beat in the lightly-whisked eggs, the vanilla essence and melted chocolate. Lastly stir in the flour, baking powder and nuts. Spread the mixture in an 8-inch square tin and bake in a moderate oven for approximately 30–35 minutes. Cut into 2-inch squares for serving.

CHERRY BUNS

4 oz margarine	½ teaspoon baking powder
3 oz sugar	a pinch salt
2 eggs	2 oz glace cherries
4½ oz flour	a little vanilla essence

Cream the margarine and sugar thoroughly and gradually beat in the lightly-whisked eggs. With the last of the egg, add the vanilla essence, dry ingredients and chopped cherries. Two-thirds fill fluted patty tins and bake in a hot oven for 15 minutes (6, E or 425°).

CHOCOLATE AND DATE FINGERS

½ lb broken Marie biscuits	1 dessertspoon castor sugar
4 oz margarine	3 dessertspoons cocoa
1 dessertspoon golden syrup	2 oz chopped dates
pink water icing made from 3 oz icing sugar to decorate	

Toast the broken biscuits in the oven, then crush with a rolling pin. Next melt the margarine, syrup and sugar in a saucepan. Stir in the cocoa, biscuit crumbs and the chopped dates. Press the mixture into a small, square sandwich tin so that it is approximately 1/2-inch thick. The tin should be lined with greased paper. Put aside until firm.

When set turn out of the tin. Spread the top with pink water icing and, when set, cut into small fingers. If wished the little cakes may be decorated still further with silver balls or other simple device.

CHOCOLATE CRISPIES

8 oz dark chocolate   *approx 2 oz cornflakes*
1/2 teaspoon instant coffee

Melt the chocolate in a bowl placed over a pan of hot water. Then stir in the instant coffee and the cornflakes. Put out in small rough heaps on to a baking tray and put aside to set.

COBURG CAKES

Traditionally, coburg cakes are made in patty tins, preferably fluted, which have been decorated after greasing with a split almond. They should be served with the almond side uppermost.

3 oz margarine   *5 oz flour*
2 oz castor sugar   *1/2 teaspoon baking powder*
1 teaspoon golden syrup   *1 teaspoon ground ginger*
1 teaspoon treacle   *a pinch of salt*
1 egg   *a few split almonds to decorate*

Cream the margarine and sugar, and gradually beat in the syrup, treacle, and whisked egg. Lastly, lightly stir in the sieved dry ingredients.

Meanwhile have fluted patty tins greased and decorate the bottom of each with a split almond. Divide the cake mixture around and bake in a fairly hot oven for approximately 15 minutes (6, E or 425°).

COCONUT AND APRICOT FINGERS

4 oz margarine   1½ breakfast cups flour
4 oz castor sugar   vanilla essence
1 egg   a little apricot jam for spreading

Coconut mixture :

1 egg   4 oz castor sugar
3 oz coconut

Cream the margarine and sugar until light. Then beat in the whisked egg and vanilla essence. Lastly, stir in the flour—the final consistency being stiff. Spread this mixture in a swiss-roll tin. Spread the apricot jam on top.

Next prepare the coconut mixture :—whisk the egg and fold in the coconut and sugar. Spread over the jam and bake all in a moderate oven for 25–30 minutes. Cut into fingers for serving.

COCONUT AND CHOCOLATE FINGERS

an 8 oz slab of baker's chocolate
cherries and chopped walnuts sufficient to sprinkle over the chocolate

Coconut mixture :

1 egg   4 oz castor sugar
3 oz fine coconut

Place the slab of chocolate in a shallow tin measuring approximately 9 by 6 inches and put in a very moderate oven to soften. When melted take from the oven and shake the tin a little from side to side to cause the chocolate to spread. While still soft, cover with a generous sprinkling of chopped cherries and walnuts.

Next combine the ingredients for the coconut mixture and spread on top of all. Press lightly into the chocolate using the back of a fork. Continue cooking in a moderate oven for a further 10 minutes. The coconut should be a golden colour. Cut into fingers when cold.

COCONUT GEMS

2 whites of egg
8 oz castor sugar
2 teaspoons lemon juice

4 oz coconut
vanilla essence

Whisk the whites of egg until stiff and gradually beat in the castor sugar. Lastly fold in the coconut, lemon juice and the vanilla essence. Put out in small, rough heaps on to a baking sheet which has been greased and dusted with flour. Bake, like meringues, in a slow oven for $1\frac{1}{2}$–2 hours ($\frac{1}{4}$, A or 300°).

COCONUT KISSES

1 tin sweetened condensed milk
$\frac{1}{2}$ lb coconut

1 dessertspoon vanilla essence
carmine and green colouring

Combine the sweetened condensed milk with the coconut and vanilla essence. Divide in two and colour, half pink and half green. Then put with a teaspoon into small rough heaps on to a greased tray. The mixture should be stiff enough with coconut to hold its shape. Bake in a cool oven until slightly browned and firm. This quantity makes approximately 40 little cakes.

COCONUT SPECIALS

6 oz margarine
2 dessertspoons cocoa
1 breakfast-cup flour
1 breakfast-cup coconut

1 breakfast-cup cornflakes (slightly crushed)
$\frac{1}{2}$ breakfast-cup sugar
1 teaspoon baking powder

Chocolate icing:

4 oz icing sugar
1 dessertspoon cocoa

boiling water

Melt the margarine and stir in the remainder of the ingredients. Mix thoroughly and press into a greased swiss-roll tin. Bake in a moderate oven for approximately 20 minutes. Ice while still fresh from the oven. When cold cut into fingers.

COCONUT AND WALNUT BARS

Shortbread mixture:

4 oz margarine	4 oz castor sugar
5 oz flour	

Nut layer:

2 eggs	a pinch of salt
a little vanilla essence	1/4 teaspoon baking powder
8 oz soft brown sugar	4 oz coconut
1 tablespoon flour	4 oz chopped walnuts

Prepare the shortbread mixture first by crumbing the margarine into the flour. Add the sugar and turn into a greased swiss-roll tin. Press flat with the back of a spoon. Then partially bake in a moderate oven.

Next prepare the nut mixture:—beat the two eggs until light. Add the vanilla, sugar, flour, salt and baking powder. Beat until smooth. Lastly stir in the nuts and pour over the shortbread base. Continue cooking for another 20–30 minutes. Cool a little and cut into fingers. These cakes are best when eaten a day or so old.

COFFEE BUNS

These buns are good when eaten with a cup of coffee—hence their name.

1/4 lb margarine	1/2 teaspoon baking soda
1/4 lb soft brown sugar	1/2 teaspoon cream of tartar
1 egg	4 oz currants
1/2 lb flour	

Cream the margarine and sugar and beat in the whisked egg. Lastly add the sieved dry ingredients and the fruit. The consistency should be stiff. Shape into small balls and arrange on a baking sheet. Brush with egg and bake in a fairly hot oven for approximately 15 minutes. When correctly baked they should be crisp on the outside. This quantity makes from 2–2 1/2 dozen little cakes.

CUP CAKES

Cup cakes are always popular and only simple ingredients and technique are necessary to produce a pretty range of cakes using the one basic mixture.

4 oz margarine
4 oz castor sugar
2 eggs

4 oz flour
¼ teaspoon baking powder

Cream the margarine and sugar thoroughly and beat in the whisked eggs. With the last of the egg add the flour and baking powder. Divide around paper baking cases, two-thirds full and bake in a fairly hot oven for 15 minutes (6, E or 400°). When cool they may be finished by one or more of the following methods:—

BUTTERFLY CAKES are probably the best known variety. Choose cakes which are quite flat on top and, with a sharp knife, cut a thin slice from the top of each cake. Cut this piece in two again. Spread the cake with jam and pipe a generous star of whipped cream in the centre. Replace the two half-slices of cake butterfly fashion, and dust with icing sugar.

CROWN CAKES. A pretty variation of the above is to make what are called "crown" cakes. Again cut a thin slice from the top of each cake, but this time cut in 4 or 6 even-sized pieces. Spread each cake with jam and pipe a high star of whipped cream in the centre. Then replace the pieces showing the cream in the middle. Decorate with a tiny piece of cherry and dust with icing sugar.

BASKET CAKES are made by once more removing a slice from the top of each cake. Spread the cake with jam and pipe with whipped cream—rather more generously to one side. Replace the slice of cake at a pretty angle to show off the cream. Finish with green cake decoration or cherry and dust with icing sugar.

CORK CAKES. Using a small cutter, ½-inch across, cut a cork shaped piece from the top of each cake. An éclair pipe is ideal for this purpose, while even an apple corer will suffice. Fill the bottom of the cavity with jam, pipe with a star of whipped cream and replace the cork at a rather jaunty angle. Dust with icing sugar.

ICED CUP CAKES. If there is a little rim of the paper case above the level of the cake then it is a simple matter to ice it with water icing. Make up 2–3 oz icing sugar into water icing and using a teaspoon, run a little over the top of each cake. The paper case will prevent the icing running down the sides and looking messy. Decorate with a silver ball, cherry and angelica or a piece of walnut.

CURRANT SQUARES

Pastry:

9 oz flour	*³/₄ oz castor sugar*
¹/₂ teaspoon salt	*egg to bind*
6 oz margarine	

Filling:

2 cooking apples	*4 oz sugar*
8 oz currants	*the grated rind of 1 lemon and a*
2 oz chopped candied peel	*little juice*

Make the pastry first:—rub the fat into the flour and salt. Add the sugar and mix to a stiff dough with part of a beaten egg. Turn on to a floured board and divide into two pieces. Use half to line a swiss-roll tin.

Next prepare the filling:—peel and chop the apples and combine with the other ingredients. Spread over the pastry and cover with the second piece. Brush with egg. Bake in a moderate oven for approximately 40 minutes (5, D or 375°). Cut into squares.

DATE CHEWS

Full of fruit and nuts and good to eat. Keep these little cakes small since they are so rich.

1 oz margarine	*1 tablespoon sugar*
¹/₂ lb chopped walnuts	*1 tablespoon self-raising flour*
¹/₂ lb chopped dates	*1 egg*

Melt the margarine and add all the other ingredients. Mix thoroughly and press into an 8-inch square sandwich tin. Bake in a moderately heated oven for 40 minutes. Cut into fingers and dust with castor sugar.

DATE FINGERS

4 oz flakemeal or porridge oats	*4 oz margarine*
4 oz flour	*2 oz soft brown sugar*
½ reaspoon baking soda	

Date filling:

½ lb dates	*a little water*
2 oz sugar	

Commence by making the filling:—chop the dates and put into a saucepan with the sugar and a little water. Stew together until reduced to a soft paste which will be easy to spread.

Next prepare the flakemeal mixture:—cut and rub the margarine into the flakemeal, flour and baking soda. Add the sugar. The mixture should resemble crumbs. Press half this mixture into an 8-inch square tin. Spread with the date filling and cover with the remainder of the flakemeal crumbs. Press well together and bake in a moderate oven for 30–40 minutes (5, D or 375°). Cut into fingers.

DEEP RIVER CHOCOLATE FINGERS

A friend who lives in Deep River, Ontario, sent me this excellent recipe for chocolate fingers, hence its curious name.

First mixture:

5 oz plain sweet biscuits	*1 beaten egg*
4 oz margarine	*1 teaspoon vanilla essence*
1½ oz castor sugar	*2 oz coconut*
3 tablespoons cocoa	*2 oz chopped walnuts*

Second mixture:

2 oz margarine	*2 tablespoons custard powder*
6 oz icing sugar	*5 tablespoons hot water*

4 oz dark chocolate   2 oz margarine

Begin by crushing the biscuits with a rolling pin, then put the margarine, sugar and cocoa in a saucepan and stir over a gentle heat until smooth. Stir in the egg and vanilla essence. Remove from the heat and add the crushed biscuits, coconut and chopped walnuts. Press the mixture into a greased swiss-roll tin and put in a cool place to set.

When firm prepare the second mixture :—cream the margarine and gradually work in the other three ingredients. Spread smoothly over the first mixture. Again leave aside in a cool place to firm.

Lastly prepare the third mixture :—melt the chocolate and the margarine together and spread like an icing on top of the cream mixture. When firm cut into finger pieces.

DESSERT CAKES

Troublesome perhaps, but so pretty and delicious that this is forgotten in one's satisfaction with the results.

6 oz margarine   6 oz flour
1½ oz icing sugar

Filling :

black or green grapes and a little hot, sieved apricot jam

Cream the margarine with the sieved icing sugar until it is really soft. Then gradually add the flour. It is most important to keep the mixture soft. Put into a forcing bag fitted with a large-sized star icing tube. Then pipe into patty tins—at first in a spiral starting in the centre and finishing with a circle of stars round the edge to make a pretty case. Stand in a cool place to firm before baking. Cook in a slow oven until a light biscuit colour (3, C or 350°). Remove from the patty tins with care and when required, the little cakes should be filled as follows:—

Cut the grapes in two and remove the seeds. Add to the hot sieved apricot jam and stir lightly so that they become coated. Then lift from the jam and arrange attractively in the cases—round side up and in a pyramid shape. The grapes should glisten with the glaze and prove refreshing to eat.

Note : In season strawberries also make a good filling for dessert cakes.

FIG. 12. *Dessert Cakes.*
(I) Pipe the mixture into patty tins—at first in a spiral and finishing with
a circle of stars round the edge
(II) Troublesome perhaps, but so pretty and delicious that this is forgotten in
one's satisfaction with the results

JAPANESE CAKES

Japanese cakes are prepared from a macaroon mixture which is baked in the form of a thin sheet, and cut into circles. The scraps are then crisped in the oven, and crushed. These, together with coffee-butter icing, are used as a finishing for the little cakes.

If any difficulty lies in the making of Japanese cakes it is in the preliminary baking of the macaroon mixture. If this is allowed to become over-cooked the cakes will be unpleasantly tough to eat. So remember to bake it carefully and only long enough to give it cohesion and a golden colour.

Macaroon mixture:
- 3 whites of egg
- 6 oz ground almonds
- 6 oz castor sugar

Coffee butter icing:
- 2 oz margarine
- 3 oz icing sugar
- coffee essence to flavour

Pink water icing to decorate:
- 1 tablespoon icing sugar
- carmine
- boiling water

First prepare a swiss-roll tin by lining it with greaseproof paper and greasing it thoroughly. Olive oil is probably the best fat to use for this purpose.

Then proceed to make the macaroon mixture:—whip the whites of egg until light but not stiff, and fold in the castor sugar and the ground almonds. Spread evenly in the prepared tin. Sometimes it is necessary to dip the knife in cold water in order to get the mixture fairly smooth. Bake in a moderate oven until it is a golden colour and just set (5, D or 375°). Take from the oven and cut into small rounds with a plain cutter. One measuring $1\frac{1}{4}$–$1\frac{1}{2}$ inches across is suitable. Break the scraps into tiny pieces and return to the oven to crisp out. Then crush them with a rolling pin as one would bread raspings.

Next prepare the butter icing in the usual way. Use it to sandwich two circles of the macaroon mixture together. Spread the butter icing on the sides and roll in the crumbs; cover the top also, and again toss in the crumbs. At this stage the little cake has the appearance of a miniature fish cake. This illusion is banished, however, by the tiny spot of pink water icing which adorns the centre. Make the water icing in a cup, for very

FIG. 13 *Japanese Cakes.*

(I)   A macaroon mixture is baked in the form of a thin sheet and cut into circles

(II) *Japanese Cakes.* Spread the butter icing on the sides and roll in the macaroon crumbs, cover the top also, and again toss in the crumbs

(III) *Japanese Cakes.* Pipe a bead of pink water icing in the centre of each little cake

little is required, and either pipe it on the cakes, or drop it in position from the point of a tea-spoon. No more than a drop the size of a pea should decorate each little cake.

PASTRY CASES

Good pastry cases are always useful and lend themselves to a variety of fillings. The following recipe is particularly recommended because of its simplicity and excellent eating qualities. The quantity given should make approximately $1-1\frac{1}{2}$ dozen cases, which will keep in a tin, to be filled as desired later.

4 oz margarine	*1 dessertspoon milk*
1½ oz castor sugar	*6 oz flour*

Cream the margarine and sugar together. Add the milk and gradually work in the flour. Roll out on a floured board. Cut into circles and use to line patty tins. Prick and bake in a moderate oven until a light biscuit colour (3, C or 350°).

Suggested fillings are as follows:—

APPLE CREAMS: Fill each case with a spoonful of stewed apple and pipe with a generous star of whipped cream. To be at their best apple creams depend largely on the quality of the stewed fruit. The apples should be stewed until mealy, well-sweetened and flavoured with clove. Sometimes, too, a little carmine is an improvement.

BANANA CREAMS: Put a little raspberry jam in the bottom of each case and two-thirds fill with the sliced banana. Level with whipped cream and spread the top of each cake with apricot-coloured water icing. Finish with a sprinkling of green cake decoration, or a little toasted flaked almonds.

CHOCOLATE CREAMS:

1 oz margarine	*6 squares melted chocolate*
1 tablespoon golden syrup	*vanilla essence*

Cream the margarine with the syrup and gradually beat in the warm melted chocolate. Flavour with vanilla. Pour into the pastry cases and sprinkle the top with chopped nuts or decorate with whipped cream.

PINEAPPLE CREAMS: Two-thirds fill each case with crushed or chopped pineapple drained free from liquid. Level with whipped cream and then spread the top of each cake with yellow-coloured water icing made using the boiled pineapple juice. Decorate with a sprinkling of green cake decoration.

PEPPERMINT STICKS
good with a cup of coffee

6 oz margarine	*3 dessertspoons cocoa*
1 breakfast-cup flour	*1/2 teaspoon peppermint essence*
1 breakfast-cup coconut	*1 teaspoon baking powder*
1/2 breakfast-cup sugar	*1 breakfast-cup cornflakes*

Peppermint butter icing:
3 oz margarine	*Peppermint essence*
4 oz icing sugar	

Decoration:
1 oz dark chocolate	*1 tablespoon margarine*

Melt the margarine and add all the other ingredients except the cornflakes. Mix well and then stir in the lightly-crushed cereal. Press into a shallow tin so that the mixture is rather more than 1/4-inch thick. Bake in a moderate oven for approximately 20 minutes. When cold spread with the peppermint-flavoured butter icing, leaving the surface attractively rough.

Now prepare the ingredients for the decoration:—cream the margarine and gradually beat in the melted chocolate. The mixture should be quite runny. Put into a paper icing bag—no pipe being necessary. Snip a small hole in the bag and "drizzle" the chocolate mixture at random over the white icing. When firm cut into neat, narrow fingers.

PINEAPPLE CREAM CAKES

A short description is all that is necessary to help cooks make these attractive cakes.

Using a small plain cutter cut circles from a 1/4-inch thick piece of sponge or genoese sponge. These are then piled with a fifty-fifty mixture of chopped glacé pineapple and whipped cream. Coat all with pineapple water icing and decorate with a tiny piece of glacé pineapple. Serve in small paper cases.

QUEEN CAKES

4 oz margarine	*¼ teaspoon baking powder*
4 oz castor sugar	*the rind of ½ lemon*
2 eggs	*4 oz currants*
4 oz flour	

Cream the margarine and sugar thoroughly. Beat in the lightly-whisked eggs and, with the last of the egg, add the flour, baking powder, lemon rind and fruit. Two-thirds fill greased patty tins and bake in a fairly hot oven for 15 minutes (6, E or 425°). This quantity makes approximately 1½ dozen cakes.

VERY LIGHT QUEEN CAKES

Often I prefer the following recipe which requires rather less flour than is usual, so that the resulting cakes are very spongy.

4 oz margarine	*¼ teaspoon baking powder*
4 oz castor sugar	*the rind of ½ lemon*
2 eggs	*4 oz currants*
3 oz flour	

Method: as previous recipe.

QUEEN ELIZABETH CAKE

One Christmas I was delighted to get this recipe in a letter from a friend in America. In sending it to me she told me that it had been obtained at a church bazaar, where the cake was for sale, and the story was that it was a recipe used by the Queen herself and one of her favourite cakes. Be that as it may, it makes a pleasant moist cake with an interesting icing.

Small cakes in variety

1 cup boiling water
1 cup chopped dates
1 teaspoon baking soda
1/4 cup margarine
1 1/2 cups flour
1 cup sugar

1/2 cup chopped nuts
1 teaspoon baking powder
1/2 teaspoon salt
1 teaspoon vanilla essence
1 egg

Icing:

2 tablespoons margarine
5 tablespoons soft brown sugar
5 tablespoons cream or unsweetened tinned milk

Pour the cupful of boiling water over the chopped dates and the baking soda. Put aside while preparing the remainder of the mixture.

Cut and rub the fat into the flour and add the sugar, nuts, baking powder and salt. Add the vanilla essence and the beaten egg to the date mixture and use to mix all to a soft batter. Turn into a lined and greased swiss-roll tin and bake in a moderate oven for approximately 35 minutes. When cold ice as follows:—combine the three ingredients for the icing in a small saucepan and boil together until beginning to thicken. Then spread over the cake and sprinkle with chopped toasted nuts. Serve cut into fingers.

TIGER CAKES

For Tiger cakes a rich biscuit mixture is made and rolled out rather thickly. It is cut into small rounds and baked. Two are sandwiched together with coffee-butter icing which is also used to cover the sides and top. The little cakes are finally rolled in chopped walnuts. Correctly speaking each should be decorated with a bead of caramel, but if preferred, something simpler will suffice.

3 oz margarine
1/2 oz castor sugar

4 oz flour

Coffee butter icing:

3 oz margarine
4 oz icing sugar

coffee essence to flavour
chopped walnuts

Caramel to decorate :

   2 oz granulated sugar and a little water

Make the biscuits first :—cream the margarine with the sugar and gradually work in the flour. Turn on to a floured board, roll out about $\frac{1}{4}$-inch thick and cut into small rounds with a plain cutter. Bake in a moderate oven (5, D or 375°).

Prepare the coffee-butter icing in the usual way and use to sandwich two biscuits together. Spread on the sides and roll in toasted chopped walnuts. Spread also, over the top and dip again in nuts.

Prepare the caramel by boiling the sugar with the minimum of water until golden and then, working quickly, drop a tiny bead of this on top of each little cake.

TRUFFLE CAKES

6 oz cake crumbs
4 oz castor sugar
2 oz ground almonds

a little sherry to flavour
apricot jam to bind

To finish :

   some melted baker's chocolate
   chocolate vermicelli
   diamonds of angelica

Sieve the cake crumbs and combine with the sugar and the ground almonds. Flavour with sherry and bind into a stiff paste using apricot jam. Form into small balls.

Using two forks, dip into the melted baker's chocolate and then toss in the chocolate vermicelli. Decorate the top of each with a diamond of angelica. Dust with icing sugar and serve in a small paper case.

Note : If preferred orange flavouring may be used instead of sherry when making the truffle cakes. In this case add a little grated rind and some juice to the mixture instead of the wine.

FIG. 14. *Truffle Cakes.*
Using two forks, dip into melted baker's chocolate and then toss
in chocolate vermicelli

VIENNESE TARTLETS

Viennese tartlets, like shortbread, are all the better for being made with butter.
The mixture should be made so soft and light that it can be piped using a savoy bag and
meringue pipe.

·8 oz ·butter
2 oz icing sugar

8 oz flour
a little raspberry jam or redcurrant
jelly for decorating

Cream the butter with the sieved icing sugar until very soft. This is important,
otherwise the mixture may prove difficult to pipe. Then gradually work in the flour.

Transfer the mixture to a forcing bag fitted with a large star pipe and pipe into patty tins using a circular motion to give a swirl slightly hollow in the centre. Put aside for at least an hour to firm before cooking. Bake in a moderate oven until a light biscuit colour (3, C or 350°).

To finish, dredge with icing sugar and pipe a bead of red jam or jelly into the well in the centre of each.

This quantity should make approximately $1\frac{1}{2}$ dozen tartlets.

WALNUT FANCIES

Pastry:

6 oz flour	*1 oz castor sugar*
4 oz margarine	*cold water to mix*

Filling:

2 oz margarine	*2 oz chopped walnuts*
2 oz castor sugar	*1 small egg*

Water icing:

2–3 oz icing sugar and boiling water to mix

Make the rich short crust pastry in the usual way and use to line patty tins.

Next prepare the walnut filling:—cream the margarine and the sugar together. Beat in the whisked egg and lastly add the chopped walnuts. Divide around the lined patty tins and bake in a moderate oven for 15–20 minutes (400°, D, or 5).

When cold, coat the top of each cake with water icing and decorate with a small piece of walnut.

Sometimes, too, half the cakes look well iced with a chocolate icing.

This quantity should make approximately $1\frac{1}{2}$ dozen little cakes.

SWEET NONSENSE

PETITS Fours and other dainty morsels have a place of their own—they bedeck the special occasion or are useful when the gesture of hospitality is all that is required in the way of catering. Naturally they should be attractive in appearance and delicious to nibble. In this country we have, on the whole, adopted the French name for these miniature cakes or biscuits, but some confectioners still use the old English name—Rout Biscuits—which were said to have originally been served at the rout parties of earlier days.

Rout Biscuits or Petits Fours have much in common—they are both small and dainty, they are frequently made from an almond mixture but, if there is a difference, it is perhaps that the French tend to use a forcing bag and pipe to get their effects, while the English rout biscuit is often modelled by hand.

Many favourite recipes for biscuits and small cakes will pass for Petits Fours if they are rich, toothsome, attractive and above all, kept very small. Apart from these there are a host of special recipes only suitable as Petits Fours and a selection of the best follow:—

ALMOND PETITS FOURS

3 whites of egg
4 oz castor sugar
flaked almonds, cherries, angelica and even currants to decorate

8 oz ground almonds
almond essence

Whisk the whites of egg until frothy and stir in the sugar, ground almonds and almond essence. The consistency should be fairly stiff. Beat well and then transfer to a forcing bag fitted with a meringue star pipe. Pipe out on to rice paper in the form of stars, fingers, whirls and "S" and "C" scrolls, and decorate prettily with shreds of almonds, cherry, angelica leaves and currants. These are best left aside for a while before baking, perhaps even overnight, when they should be lightly brushed with egg and toasted quickly in a hot oven (7, F, or 450°).

This quantity makes approximately 30 petits fours.

ENGLISH ROUT BISCUITS

English Rout Biscuits are modelled from a form of marzipan made entirely with castor sugar and mixed with yolks of egg. This gives the mixture the texture and richness which is characteristic of these little biscuits. The marzipan may be coloured before use and can be shaped in a great variety of ways. A good selection is described, but the cook's own ingenuity will probably add to the list.

¼ *lb ground almonds*	*2–3 yolks of egg*
¼ *lb castor sugar*	*almond essence*

Combine the ground almonds with the castor sugar and flavour with the almond essence. Then mix all to a pliable paste of modelling consistency. Avoid over-working it or it becomes oily. Make up into little biscuits as follows; the quantity in the recipe should make approximately thirty.

CHERRY HORNS. Roll out some of the rout paste fairly thin and cut into circles using a 1½ inch cutter. Brush the centre with egg, lay half a cherry on top and draw the marzipan round horn fashion. Arrange on a greased and floured tray and put aside for several hours to firm. Brush with egg and bake in a hot oven just sufficiently long to flash the edges with brown (7, F or 450°).

ROUT RINGS. Colour some of the paste either pink or green and roll out fairly thickly. Then cut into small rings using two plain cutters of nearly the same size. Bake as already described and finish with a little white water icing and four silver balls placed at the four points of the compass.

ALMOND ROUT BISCUITS. Colour the rout paste, and roll out and cut into small fancy biscuits. Brush with egg and stick a split almond on top. Flash off in a hot oven as before.

CHOCOLATE STICKS. Using coloured rout paste roll out fairly thickly and cut into neat sticks. Bake for a short time without brushing with egg and, when cold, dip the tips in melted baker's chocolate and then in chocolate vermicelli.

WALNUT BON-BONS. Roll some coloured rout paste into small balls. Stick a half walnut on either side. After standing, brush the top of each with egg and bake in a sharp oven for a few minutes.

LITTLE LOAVES. Shape some plain rout paste into little balls, flatten slightly and mark the top with the back of a knife in the form of a cross. After standing, brush with egg and finish off in a hot oven.

Other shapes may be made similarly such as baton, oval or cottage loaf style.

BOULES de NEIGE

1 oz hazel nuts	*2 oz icing sugar*
1 oz ground almonds	*a little white of egg to bind*

For finishing :

A little white of egg and some sieved icing sugar.

Grind the hazel nuts in a nut mill or the liquidiser of the mixing machine. Then combine with the ground almonds and sieved icing sugar. Mix to a stiff paste with a little beaten white of egg. The mixture is rather similar to almond paste. Divide into ten even-sized pieces and roll each into a ball. Brush with a little beaten white of egg and roll in sieved icing sugar. Put in little paper sweet cases and bake in a very moderate oven until puffed. This will take between 5 and 10 minutes. Suggested oven temperatures being 3, C or 350°.

CARAMEL CHESTNUTS

6 oz prepared chestnuts	*2 oz castor sugar*
1 tea-cup milk	*1 tablespoon brandy*
3 oz sieved cake crumbs	*1 tablespoon cream*
rice flour for shaping.	

Caramel :

6 oz sugar and a little cold water

Make a slit in approximately ½ lb chestnuts, place in a pan of cold water, bring to the boil and boil for 10 minutes. Take from the water, a few at a time, and remove

131

FIG. 15. *Petits Fours in Variety.*
Reading across the picture: (1) Conutines (2) Cherry Horns (3) Little
Almond Cakes (4) Rum Truffles (5) Ginger Crowns (6) Almond Petits Fours (7) Cherry and
Almond Balls

both the outer and inner skin. Then put in a small saucepan with the milk, and stew until tender. Sieve and weigh off 6 oz of chestnut. Put in a bowl and add the other ingredients. Shape into small balls using a little rice flour to prevent the mixture sticking. Leave aside for some time to dry and form a skin.

Next prepare the caramel :—Put the sugar in a small strong saucepan and add 2–3 tablespoons water. Stir over a gentle heat until dissolved. Then stir in a pinch of cream of tartar, and remove the spoon and bring to the boil. Boil until a light golden colour. Then dip the little balls into the caramel. Lay on a greased tin. Sprinkle with green cake decoration while still sticky and serve in a paper case.

These cakes are for eating immediately, since the caramel is so apt to go sticky.

CHERRY AND ALMOND BALLS

A glacé cherry is used for the centre of these pretty and delectable little morsels. It is enveloped in marzipan, rolled in flaked almonds, toasted and finally, decorated with a small bead of glistening caramel. The cakes are prettiest if the marzipan is used in two shades—for example a combination of natural colour and green makes a pleasant contrast with the rich red of the core.

4 oz icing sugar
4 oz ground almonds
almond essence
white of egg to bind

green colouring
14–16 glacé cherries
flaked almonds to finish

Caramel :

1 oz sugar and a little water

Sieve the icing sugar and combine with the ground almonds. Flavour with the essence and, using white of egg, mix all to a soft pliable paste. Use approximately half of this mixture to mould a thin layer round each cherry. Colour the remainder green and soften with white of egg to give a sticky paste. With the aid of two forks, roll the cherry balls in this. Lift out on to the flaked almonds and toss through these. Arrange on a baking sheet and brown quickly in a hot oven (6, E or 400°).

Make the caramel in a small saucepan and, working quickly, drop a little in the centre of each cake. Sprinkle with green cake decoration and serve in paper cases.

CONUTINES

Conutines consist of a mixture very like almond paste, but containing a proportion of coconut. This mixture is made into small balls which are, in turn, dipped in royal icing, rolled in coconut and, when the icing is hard, baked. They make unusual little cakes, and are popular with all who sample them.

1 oz icing sugar
1 oz coconut
3 oz ground almonds
4 oz castor sugar

a little vanilla essence
1 yolk of egg
if necessary, a little water to bind

Royal icing :

    4 oz icing sugar and a little white of egg
    extra coconut for coating

Pink water icing :

    1 tablespoon icing sugar
    carmine
    boiling water

Prepare the almond and coconut mixture first. Sieve the icing sugar and mix with the other dry ingredients. Flavour with vanilla and mix to a soft, but not sticky, paste, using the yolk of egg and a little water if necessary. Shape into balls. This quantity should make from 16–18, and it is perhaps necessary to emphasise that they should be small since the icing and coconut will increase their size in due course.

Next prepare the royal icing :—Sieve the icing sugar, and beat in sufficient white of egg to give a creamy coating consistency. Dip the balls in this and then toss in coconut. Avoid patting in too much coconut as this tends to spoil the eating qualities of the cakes. Place on a baking sheet and set aside until the next day. Toast prettily in a hot oven (6, E or 400°). Serve in paper cases dusted with icing sugar and decorated, if wished, with a bead of pink water icing.

DUTCH MACAROONS

The distinctive feature of Dutch macaroons is the lovely smile down the centre of each one. This is obtained by an interesting trick. After shaping, the macaroons are left in a warm place until they form a thick skin. This is then cut through from end to end with a sharp knife. When the macaroons are in the oven the centre mixture bubbles through giving them a most attractive and appetising appearance.

6 oz icing sugar   *almond essence*
2 oz ground almonds   *approximately 1–1½ whites of egg*

Sieve the icing sugar and combine with the ground almonds. Flavour with almond essence and mix to a thick creamy consistency with the lightly-whisked whites of egg. The mixture, if correct, should flow level without spreading. Place in a large forcing

FIG. 16. *Dutch Macaroons.*
(I)—after shaping, the macaroons are left in a warm place until they
form a thick skin. This is then cut through from end to end with a sharp knife
(II)—when the macaroons are in the oven the centre mixture bubbles through
the cut in a most attractive way

bag, fitted with a $\frac{1}{4}$-inch plain pipe, and pipe into small oval shapes on to sheets of rice paper. Put aside in a warm place for one or two days until a thick skin has formed. Then, using a sharp knife, make a clean cut from end to end of each biscuit. Bake in a moderate oven until golden (325°, B, or 2).

If wished, two of these macaroons may be sandwiched together with coffee-flavoured butter icing.

GINGER CROWNS

These little cakes are particularly delicious to eat, and consist of a combination of marzipan and finely chopped ginger. They are fashioned somewhat after the shape of a crown and the centre is iced with a ginger-flavoured water icing. If this seems too troublesome use the same basic mixture and simplify the shape as you please.

2 oz ground almonds	*1–2 yolks of egg*
2 oz castor sugar	*a little syrup from the jar of ginger*
1 tablespoon finely chopped pre-served ginger	

Icing:

2 tablespoons icing sugar	*a little boiling water*
1 teaspoon ginger syrup	

Decoration:

small pieces of preserved ginger.

Put the ground almonds, castor sugar and chopped ginger in a bowl. Stir in the ginger syrup and mix all to a stiff paste with the yolks of egg.

Divide the mixture roughly in half and, from one piece, shape small balls like marbles. Roll the other piece out fairly thinly and cut into strips, the width being a little greater than the diameter of the ball of mixture—one side of this strip should be cut with a fluted edge if possible. Wrap these around the little balls in such a way as to make miniature "crowns".

These are best left overnight before baking, then brown quickly by placing in a hot oven for a few minutes. Lastly fill the centre of each crown with a little ginger-flavoured water icing and decorate with a small piece of ginger.

Neat workers will appreciate the hint that the water icing is best piped into the centre of each little cake. Use a paper icing bag with a small hole cut in the point instead of a pipe.

LITTLE ALMOND CAKES
delicious and so easy to make

This simple mixture plays tricks in the oven. It is put from a teaspoon into little paper cases and baked in a moderately-heated oven. At first it rises but, since there is no flour, it falls again to give a little case of almond mixture suitable for filling.

For variety, ground Brazil nuts might be used instead of the ground almonds, and the filling may be varied too.

3 oz margarine   *4 oz ground almonds*
3 oz castor sugar

Filling:

apricot jam
whipped, sweetened and flavoured cream to decorate

Cream the margarine and sugar together and gradually work in the ground almonds. Then divide around approximately $2\frac{1}{2}$–3 dozen little paper sweet cases. Bake in a moderate oven for about 10–15 minutes. Suggested oven temperatures being 3, C or 350°.

When cold peel off the paper case. Before serving fill with a little good quality apricot jam and pipe with a star of whipped cream.

RUM TRUFFLES

Rum truffles are rich and delicious and combine well with a cup of coffee, while their dark colouring is in pleasant contrast to the lighter shades of the majority of petits fours.

3 oz dark chocolate	*rum to flavour*
1 yolk of egg	*chocolate vermicelli*
1 oz butter	

Melt the chocolate and stir in the yolk, butter and rum. Put aside until cool and firm enough to handle, then roll into balls. Toss these in the chocolate vermicelli and serve in paper cases.

AS LIGHT AS A FEATHER

IT is a source of great satisfaction to be able to make good rough-puff, flaky and puff pastry—pastry which is as light as air, delicately puffed and crisp to eat. The art is not difficult to acquire, but it is an achievement which must be sought after, for it comes only with practice and an attention to detail. These pastries lend themselves to the making of a number of desirable small cakes without which one's repertoire would not be complete.

SOME USEFUL HINTS

The difference between rough-puff, flaky and puff pastry largely lies in the proportion of fat used and in the different methods employed to incorporate the fat with the dough. Some cooks find they get more successful results with one method than another.

In making any of these pastries the fat is important. It may either be butter—delicious and easiest to work with, margarine (or a mixture of margarine and lard), or cooking fat. If two fats are used they should be blended evenly together before commencing work.

It is also worth noting that the fat and the dough should both be about the same consistency. Thus, if the fat is soft owing to the weather, then the dough should be soft too. Conversely, if the fat is firm the dough should be mixed a little stiffer. The pastry is much less likely to stick when rolling if this rule is observed. Incidentally, a fairly soft, kindly dough usually gives the lightest pastry.

As you will know these pastries depend for their lightness on the rollings and foldings given and it is important to incorporate as much cold air as possible in this way. With this in view, work in a cool place; dust the pastry lightly with flour before folding to prevent the layers sticking and, when folding, seal the edges by damping with a little cold water and pressing with the rolling pin. Try to avoid rolling in an excess of flour; a dry pastry brush near to hand is useful for brushing off any surplus.

ROUGH PUFF PASTRY

8 oz flour   *a little salt*
5–6 oz fat   *approx 1 gill cold water*

Sieve the flour and salt into a bowl. Add the fat and cut into pieces about the size of a walnut. Then mix all to an elastic dough with the cold water. Turn on to a floured board and roll into a long strip. Flour lightly, damp the edges and fold in three. Give a half turn and roll out again. Repeat a third time, and if the fat is still not evenly mixed through the pastry, give a fourth rolling. If possible put the pastry aside between rollings to rest and cool.

The pastry is now ready for use. It should be baked in a hot oven (9, G or 475°).

FLAKY PASTRY

8 oz flour   *a little salt*
6 oz fat   *approx 1 gill cold water*

Sieve the flour and salt into a mixing bowl. Cut and rub in one quarter of the fat and mix to an elastic dough with the cold water. Turn on to a floured board and knead lightly. Roll out into a long narrow strip. Cover two-thirds of this strip with small pats of the fat using the second quarter. Dust with flour, damp the edges and fold in three. Give a half turn and repeat with the remaining two quarters of fat. Roll out twice more—in all there are four rollings. As convenient put the pastry aside in between rollings, or at least between every second rolling.

Use as required and bake in a hot oven (9, G or 475°).

PUFF PASTRY

In the normal way puff pastry is made using equal quantities of flour and fat; the fat is incorporated by rolling and folding the pastry seven times. This is a long process, especially when it is remembered that it is advisable to put the pastry aside to rest, in a cool place, between every second rolling. The recipe which follows is a simplified one and involves the cook in only four rollings instead of the usual seven. The result is excellent being spectacular to look at and good to eat.

The method used may seem unorthodox since the fat–preferably Empire butter– is combined with a small proportion of the flour, rolled out and used to envelop a dough made with the remainder of the flour. Obviously, if this is to be an easy task it is important that the butter should be firm but pliable and the work should be carried out in a cool place using a marble slab.

The method of folding, too, is different. The pastry is given what is called a "double fold" after each rolling, and this builds up the required number of layers more quickly than the normal "single fold".

It is interesting to note that when puff pastry is ready for use 762 layers have been built up by the cook.

The method step by step :—

1. Sift $\frac{1}{2}$ lb flour on to a marble slab and divide it roughly into two parts of approximately one-third and two-thirds.

2. Put $\frac{1}{2}$ lb firm butter in a bowl and add one-third of the flour. Cut the fat into small pieces and then, using the fingers, work it into the flour as in making shortbread. Put aside in a cool place.

3. Put the remainder of the flour into the bowl, and mix to a soft elastic dough with the cold water. The dough should be similar in consistency to the butter and flour mixture. Knead until smooth.

4. Sprinkle the marble slab with flour and pat the butter and flour mixture into a neat rectangular shape. Roll into a long strip.

5. Next roll the piece of dough so that it is equal in size to half the strip of fat and flour.

6. Place it on one end of the long strip and fold it over so that the dough is neatly enclosed in a casing of butter.

7. Give the pastry a half turn, so that the open ends are back and front and roll into a long strip.

8. Dust lightly with flour and fold the two ends in to the centre of the strip; then fold in two. This should give a total of 4 layers.

9. Seal the ends and again give a half turn.

10. Repeat the rolling and folding in all four times, allowing a rest between the second and third rollings or, more frequently, if the pastry is difficult to handle.

The pastry is now ready for use. When it is being cut, it is a good idea to dip the knife (or cutter) into boiling water. This may sound strange, but is much more successful than dipping it in flour.

Finally, always give puff pastry a rest in a cool place before baking. This will be found to do much to prevent shrinkage. Bake in a fairly hot oven, suggested temperatures being 475°, G or 9 for small things, and slightly lower temperatures for bigger items.

APPLE TURNOVERS

Apple turnovers are delicious, but only too often they are spoiled in the baking if the sweetened fruit juice boils out and burns. This can be avoided, as suggested in the following recipe, by omitting to add any sugar to the apple. When the turnovers are baked, they should be dusted thickly with icing sugar. Surprisingly enough, no one will notice the original omission.

This is what you do; roll some flaky or puff pastry out fairly thin, and cut into large circles. Peel and slice some apples finely, and put a little on each circle of pastry. Brush the edges with beaten egg and fold over. Place on a wet baking sheet, and put in a cool place for half an hour. Bake in a fairly hot oven and serve while hot, thickly dusted with icing sugar.

BANBURY CAKES
still made and sold in Banbury

½ lb rough-puff or flaky pastry

Filling:

1 oz margarine	*2 oz soft brown sugar*
½ oz flour	*grated nutmeg*
4 oz currants	*2 tablespoons rum*
1 oz chopped candied peel	

Melt the margarine for the filling and stir in the flour; cook together for a couple of minutes. Then take from the heat and stir in the other ingredients. Put aside to cool.

Next roll the pastry about ¼-inch thick and cut into 3-inch circles. Put a little of the filling on each, damp the edges and draw together. Pinch firmly and turn right over. Roll lightly to give an oval shape. Mark with the back of a knife and bake in a hot oven for 20 minutes. Brush with white of egg, dust with sugar and return to the oven for a minute to dry.

As light as a feather

CONVERSATION CAKES
troublesome but delicious

6 oz puff pastry

a little raspberry jam

Filling:

1 oz margarine
1 oz castor sugar
1 oz ground almonds

1 yolk of egg
vanilla essence

Royal icing:

2 oz icing sugar
½ teaspoon flour

a little white of egg

Roll the puff pastry out thinly and cut into circles using a plain cutter. Use half these to line patty tins. Put a little raspberry jam in the bottom of each case.

Make the filling by the creaming method and divide around the patty tins. Damp the edges and use the remaining circles of pastry to cover. With a palette knife cover each tartlet with a creamy spreading of royal icing. Finally decorate with four thin strips of puff pastry arranged as for "noughts and crosses." This could be fiddling work if each cake was decorated separately. However if a sheet of nine or twelve patty tins is used it is an easy matter to run strips of pastry the length of the tray and so get the job done quickly. Snip the strips between each cake before baking to allow the puff pastry every opportunity to rise while in the oven.

Bake in a moderate oven for 20 minutes. Suggested oven temperatures being 6, E or 400°. This quantity should make approximately 1 dozen cakes.

COVENTRY'S OR THREE-CORNERED PUFFS

"Coventry's" is the name given to triangular or three-cornered jam puffs. They look most attractive and are good to eat if served fresh from the oven.

To make them, roll some flaky or puff pastry out very thin—about one-sixteenth of an inch—and cut into large circles. Place a little jam in the centre of each, damp the edges with water, then fold towards the centre at three places to give a triangular shape. Turn over, so that the join is underneath, brush with water and dip in castor sugar.

FIG. 17. *Conversation Cakes.*
(I) Decorate each cake with four strips of puff pastry arranged as
for "noughts and crosses". This is an easy matter if the strips are run the length and width
of the tray
(II) Delicious with their almond filling and sugary top

Put aside on baking sheets for 15–30 minutes. Then bake in a fairly hot oven for 15–20 minutes (7, F or 450°).

CREAM HORNS

Actually cream horns may very well be made using puff pastry trimmings left over from other baking. These should be rolled out thinly and cut into ribbons about 1 inch wide and 14–16 inches long. Roll these strips round horn moulds, commencing at the point and allowing each roll to overlap the previous one. During this process try to avoid stretching the pastry. Damp the end of the strip to secure it; trim also, if necessary.

Arrange the horns on a baking sheet and rest well before cooking, to prevent shrinking in the oven. Then brush the top with water and sprinkle with sugar. Bake in a fairly hot oven for approximately 20 minutes. Remove from the moulds while the pastry is still warm.

To finish, put a little raspberry jam in the bottom of each and fill with whipped cream.

ECCLES CAKES

Eccles cakes come to us from Lancashire and, in many ways, are rather similar to Banbury puffs. The most noticeable difference is one of shape—the latter being oval and the former round. In detail the filling is somewhat different too.

½ lb rough-puff, flaky or puff pastry

Filling:

1 oz margarine	1 oz soft brown sugar
4 oz currants	nutmeg
1 oz chopped candied peel	a little mixed spice

To prepare the filling melt the margarine and stir in the other ingredients. Flavour nicely with grated nutmeg and mixed spice. Put aside to cool.

Roll the pastry out about ¼-inch thick and cut in circles of approximately 3–4

145

inches diameter. Divide the filling around these, damp the edges, then gather together to seal. Pinch securely to prevent the filling oozing out and burning, and turn over. Roll lightly with a rolling pin to produce a round flat cake with the currants just beginning to show. Mark, criss-cross fashion, with the back of a knife, brush with water and dust with sugar. Bake in a hot oven for 15–20 minutes.

FRANGIPANE TARTLETS

A frangipane filling is a mixture made with ground almonds, and it has good eating qualities. It may be used in a variety of ways with puff pastry; two favourite suggestions follow:—

First of all the recipe for the frangipane filling:—

2 oz margarine	*1 egg*
2 oz castor sugar	*vanilla essence*
2 oz ground almonds	

Cream the margarine and sugar until light. Beat in the lightly-whisked egg, then the ground almonds and the vanilla essence. Use as a filling in one of the following ways:—

FRANGIPANE TARTLETS No. 1. Line patty tins with circles of thinly-rolled puff pastry. Put a little raspberry or apricot jam in the bottom of each and cover with the frangipane mixture. Bake in a moderately-hot oven for 15–20 minutes.

FRANGIPANE TARTLETS No. 2. Roll out some puff pastry fairly thinly and cut into circles with a fluted cutter. Brush half the circles with water and put a teaspoon of the frangipane filling in the centre. Cover with a second circle of pastry. After resting, brush with white of egg and sprinkle with shredded almonds. Bake in a fairly hot oven for 15–20 minutes and serve freshly-baked and dusted with icing sugar.

MILLE FEUILLES

Light as air and with as many leaves as a fat book, mille feuilles is a classic popular with all. This pastry is particularly useful to make as a means of using up puff pastry trimmings.

This is what you do; roll the puff pastry into 3 or 4 rectangular pieces of a size to fit swiss-roll tins. Place on the wet trays, prick well and put aside in a cool place to rest before baking. This is important otherwise the pastry is very apt to shrink on cooking. Bake in a fairly hot oven and when half-cooked turn each piece over on the tray and return to the oven to complete the cooking. The pastry when ready should be lightly brown, crisp but not risen a great deal.

When cold, sandwich together with a light spreading of raspberry jam and whipped cream. Press well together, if necessary under a board for a time. Then cut into generous fingers and serve dusted with icing sugar.

Alternatively, and more correctly, the slab of mille feuilles may be spread with white water icing and decorated by feathering with pink and chocolate icing. Cut into fingers when the icing is set.

MAKING ECLAIRS AND SNOWBALLS

CHOUX pastry is used for making éclairs and snowballs, and most cookery books give a standard recipe for this pastry. The one which follows is a little different and, I think, rather better. In this recipe rather more fat is used than usual and lard is recommended instead of butter and margarine. Its special merit lies in the fact that it can be relied upon to bake quite hollow, which is a great convenience when snowballs or éclairs are to be filled with cream.

CHOUX PASTRY

¼ pint water
2 oz lard
2 small eggs

2¼ oz flour
a pinch of salt

Put the water and lard into a saucepan and bring to the boil. Immediately boiling point is reached, shoot in the flour and salt from a piece of paper. Draw the pan to the side of the heat and beat until smooth using a wooden spoon. Then return to the heat and cook for three minutes, beating very thoroughly. Cool slightly before continuing. Whisk the two eggs and gradually beat into the mixture in the saucepan. This beating is hard work as the mixture is stiff. It is essential, however, and must not be skimped, since the pastry is entirely dependent on the air which is incorporated, if it is to rise. While adding the last of the egg it is important to watch the consistency of the mixture. If correct it should be soft but still capable of holding its shape. The pastry is now ready for use.

SNOWBALLS

Snowballs are easier to shape than éclairs and consist of rough teaspoonfuls of the mixture put out on to a greased baking sheet. They should be arranged a little apart as they will rise considerably.

Making eclairs and snow balls

Snowballs should be baked in a moderately hot oven, and will require approximately 20–30 minutes, according to their size. On no account should the oven door be opened during the first 15 minutes, as any draught or disturbance would cause them to collapse and be a total failure. Exact oven temperatures are as follows—gas ovens: 5 or E; electric ovens: 425°.

Superb results may be achieved when making snowballs if it can be arranged to bake them covered. It would seem that the steam which occurs during the baking and which is retained by the cover, helps them to rise. They more than double their size, are delightfully light, and completely hollow. Baking by this method needs special care however.

First of all it is necessary to improvise some method of covering the snowballs while they are in the oven. I think the simplest procedure is to use glass ovenware, or to put them out on a greased baking sheet in the usual way and to invert a deep roasting tin over them. The cover should fit fairly tightly so it may be necessary to weight it down and, of course, there should be room for each bun to expand.

Place all in a moderately hot oven. If half the mixture has been made into éclairs, as is often done, then these should be placed on the top shelf and the snowballs on the second shelf.

Snowballs which are to be baked covered require much longer to cook than those which are uncovered. I like to allow them an hour but, again, the time will depend on the size. It is important to note that one must not even peep under the cover until the pastry is set. Incidentally, this method of baking applies only to snowballs and not to éclairs.

Snowballs are usually finished with a thick dusting of icing sugar but they are also very attractive if the top is dipped into caramel. This gives them a sweet, crisp surface which is a pleasant change. The recipe is as follows:—

Caramel:

4 oz sugar	a pinch of cream of tartar
a little water	

Put the sugar into a small, strong saucepan and add only sufficient water to help it to dissolve. Place over a gentle heat and stir until clear; then stir in a pinch of cream of tartar. Remove the spoon and bring to the boil; then boil until an attractive golden colour. Remove from the heat and quickly dip the tops of the snowballs into the caramel.

ÉCLAIRS

To shape éclairs it is necessary to use a large forcing bag fitted with an éclair pipe. Put the mixture into the bag and pipe it out about $3\frac{1}{2}$ inches long. Bake in a moderate oven for approximately 20–30 minutes (5, E or 425°).

Finishing the cakes. The cakes when baked should be hollow but, if necessary, remove any soft dough from the centre of each. Fill generously with whipped cream.

Éclairs are iced using either chocolate or coffee-flavoured water icing and the recipe for the chocolate icing is as follows:—

Chocolate water icing:

3 oz icing sugar　　　　　　　　　　　　　　*boiling water to mix*
$1\frac{1}{2}$ oz dark chocolate

Sieve the icing sugar and melt the chocolate. Combine, and mix to a creamy consistency with boiling water. Beat well and use to ice the éclairs.

CAKES FOR THE STORE CUPBOARD

A LARGE cake for cutting, which will keep well, is invaluable and, as with other things, variety is always appreciated.

Some cooks feel hesitant about baking a big cake, but really this anxiety is groundless if a few simple rules are carefully followed. One aims at having a cake which is an attractive even colour, flat on top, and moist to the touch and to the palate. To get these results the cake must be correctly placed in the oven and the baking temperature and timing must be suitable. Most modern ovens are fitted with a temperature control and so guessing is eliminated. There is always, however, a slight difference from oven to oven and experience is the only guide in these circumstances. Remember the golden rule is "the larger and richer the cake the slower the oven." A big cake should always be placed on a middle or low shelf in the oven, so that it will not become too brown before it is cooked through.

When using a reliable oven I find that there is little need to be unduly careful lining the cake tin with layers of paper. One layer is quite sufficient and often I am content to line only the bottom of the tin. Greasing is also unnecessary for rich mixtures.

GENOA CAKE

The distinguishing feature of this pleasant fruit cake is the fresh flavour of lemon which pervades through a medley of currants, sultanas and raisins. It is moist and a good keeper.

½ lb butter or margarine	½ lb currants
½ lb castor sugar	½ lb sultanas
6 eggs	½ lb raisins
10 oz flour	¼ lb lemon peel
the juice and grated rind of 1 lemon	a few flaked almonds

Cream the butter and sugar thoroughly and add the eggs and flour gradually and alternately. Lastly add the lemon and the fruit. Turn into a prepared 8-inch cake tin and sprinkle the top with flaked almonds. Bake in a moderate oven for 2½ hours. Approx-imate temperature being 4, C or 350°.

SHERRY PLUM CAKE

A sherry plum cake is a pleasantly "different" type of rich fruit cake. It is excellent for storing, is moist, and suitable for use as a birthday or Christmas cake. It is, however, not so dark a cake as the plum cake suggested for use as a Christmas cake later in this book

½ lb butter or margarine	½ teaspoon baking powder
½ lb soft brown sugar	1 glass sherry
3 eggs	1½ lb currants
½ lb flour	½ lb candied lemon peel

Cream the butter and sugar thoroughly. Then add the eggs and the flour gradually and alternately, beating well between each addition; with the last of the flour beat in the sherry. Finally stir in the fruit and turn into a prepared 8-inch cake tin. Bake at 4, C or 350° for approximately 2½ hours.

DUNDEE CAKE

½ lb butter or margarine	4 oz raisins
½ lb castor sugar	4 oz sultanas
5–6 eggs	2 oz chopped candied peel
½ lb flour	3 oz ground almonds
4 oz currants	the zest of 1 orange
blanched split or shredded almonds to strew the top	

Beat the butter or margarine and the sugar to a cream. Then beat in the eggs one at a time. With the last of the egg start adding the flour. Finally add the prepared fruits. Turn the mixture into a prepared 8-inch tin, strew with almonds and bake in a mod-erate oven for approximately 2 hours (4, C or 350°).

FIG. 18. *Almond Macaroon Cake.*
Is covered with a layer of macaroon which is baked with the cake

ALMOND MACAROON CAKE

Almond macaroon cake is splendid for cutting and it has two features which are worth a comment. In the first place there is a considerable amount of angelica used in the cake itself, and this makes it very good to eat. In addition the cake is covered with a layer of macaroon, scattered with shredded almonds and together these make it more interesting and luscious.

This cake, like others in this section, is best stored for a week or ten days before cutting.

4 oz butter or margarine	1½ oz ground almonds
4 oz castor sugar	4 oz currants
2 eggs and 1 yolk	4 oz sultanas
5 oz flour	4 oz chopped angelica

Macaroon mixture:

1 white of egg	3 oz ground almonds
4 oz castor sugar	a little almond essence
¾ oz flaked almonds for the top of the cake	

Cream the butter and sugar thoroughly; then beat in the eggs and the flour alternately, adding them in small amounts, and beating each addition in well. Lastly add the fruit. Turn into a lined cake tin. One measuring 7 inches in diameter is suitable.

Next prepare the macaroon mixture. Half whisk the white of egg and fold in the other ingredients. Spread over the top of the cake and sprinkle with the flaked almonds. Cover with an inverted swiss-roll tin. Weight and bake at 4, or C, or 350° for approximately 2 hours. The cover may be removed during the last half hour.

ONE-EGG PLUM CAKE

While economical, this recipe is a worthy one. The finished cake is moist, dark, full of fruit and is popular with all who sample it.

8 oz flour	8 oz raisins
4 oz margarine	2 oz China ginger
4 oz castor sugar	1 small well-beaten egg
8 oz sultanas	¼ pint buttermilk
8 oz currants	½ teaspoon baking soda

Rub the margarine into the flour and add the sugar and fruit. Add the baking soda to the buttermilk, and use with the well-beaten egg, to combine all to give a mixture similar to that made by more conventional methods. Spread in a prepared 7-inch cake tin and bake at 4, C or 350° for 1½–2 hours.

BOILED FRUIT CAKE

Boiled fruit cake is a much more economical recipe than any of the others in this section and yet it makes a good cake for family use. The method of making it is unorthodox but it will be found very quick and labour saving.

1 cup water	*3 teaspoons mixed spice*
1/4 lb margarine	*2 cups flour*
1 cup brown sugar	*1 teaspoon baking soda*
1 cup currants	*1 egg*
1 cup sultanas	

Using a breakfast cup for measuring, put the water, margarine, sugar, fruit and spice into a saucepan and simmer for 20 minutes. Put aside to cool. When cold add the flour, baking soda and beaten egg. Mix thoroughly and turn into a prepared cake tin. Bake in a moderate oven for approximately $1\frac{1}{2}$ hours (4, C or 350°).

ALMOND CAKE

An almond cake may not sound or look very exciting but nevertheless it is a cake worth sampling because of its moist and pleasant texture and good flavour. It is also easy to make since there is no fruit to be prepared. An almond cake is similar to a Madeira cake in appearance but with the important addition of a proportion of ground almonds to the mixture. It should also be happily 'labelled' with a generous sprinkling of flaked almonds on the top

8 oz butter or margarine	*1/2 teaspoon baking powder*
8 oz castor sugar	*4 oz ground almonds*
4 eggs and a little water	*a little almond and vanilla essence*
6 oz flour	*a few flaked almonds*

Line an 8-inch cake tin, but do not grease the paper.

Next prepare the mixture. Cream the butter and sugar, and gradually beat in the lightly-whisked eggs. Lastly, add the flour, baking powder, ground almonds and a little almond and vanilla essence. Correct the consistency by beating in a little water. Spread

155

in the prepared cake tin and sprinkle the top with shredded almonds. Bake in a moderate oven at 4, C or 350°. The time required is approximately 1 hour 40 minutes.

A STORE CAKE

10 oz butter or margarine　　　　　*1 lb fruit, for example :—*
10 oz castor sugar　　　　　　　　*¼ lb raisins*
5 eggs　　　　　　　　　　　　　　*¼ lb glacé cherries*
12 oz flour　　　　　　　　　　　　*¼ lb currants*
2 oz grounds almonds　　　　　　　*¼ lb sultanas*
　　　　　　　　　　　　　　　　　　rind of half a lemon
　　　　　　　　　　　　　　　　　　1 small teaspoon vinegar

Prepare an 8–8½ inch cake tin by lining with paper. Next prepare the fruit. Cream the butter and sugar until fluffy. Add the vinegar, then beat in the eggs and flour alternately. Lastly add the fruit. Turn the mixture into the prepared cake tin and bake in a moderate oven for approximately 2½ hours (4, C or 350°).

SPICE CAKE WITH FUDGE ICING

Fudge icing is tricky but delicious and is equally good to bedeck other cakes such as a fruit mixture, walnut, or coffee and walnut cakes.

8 oz margarine　　　　　　　　　　*2 oz ground almonds*
8 oz soft brown sugar　　　　　　　*¾ teaspoon ground cloves*
4 eggs　　　　　　　　　　　　　　*½ teaspoon ground cinnamon*
8 oz flour　　　　　　　　　　　　　*¼ teaspoon baking soda*

Cream the margarine and sugar thoroughly. Gradually beat in the lightly-whisked eggs and with the last of the egg the dry ingredients. Turn the mixture into a prepared 8-inch cake tin and bake in a moderate oven for 1¾ hours, approximate temperatures being 4, C or 350°

When cold, cover the top of the cake with the following fudge icing:—

1 small tin evaporated milk	*2 oz margarine*
8 oz granulated sugar	*vanilla essence*

Put the milk, margarine and sugar into a strong saucepan and stir over a gentle heat until the sugar has dissolved. Then simmer quietly until a rich golden colour and until a little, when tested in cold water, gives a soft ball. Remove from the heat, add the vanilla essence and beat until it shows signs of thickening. Pour quickly to cover the top of the cake. Using a knife, swirl attractively and sprinkle with walnuts if liked.

Note: When icing this particular cake I find it convenient to line the sides of the tin with paper and to leave this collar in position to catch the icing and mould it to an exact fit.

PINEAPPLE AND CHERRY CAKE

This unusual and excellent cake has a beautifully moist texture, largely due to the addition of a small quantity of ground almonds. In addition the pretty green colour of the crumb looks well with the contrasting yellow and red of the glacé pineapple and cherries and the pure white of the American icing.

6 oz butter or margarine	*3 oz glacé cherries*
6 oz castor sugar	*3 oz glacé pineapple*
3 eggs	*2 oz ground almonds*
5 oz flour	*green colouring*
1 teaspoon baking powder	

American icing made using 8 oz granulated sugar to coat the cake
Decoration: pieces of glacé pineapple, cherries and silver balls.

Cream the butter (or margarine) and sugar thoroughly and gradually beat in the lightly-whisked eggs. With the last of the egg add the flour and baking powder and finally stir in the roughly chopped fruit. Colour the whole mixture a pretty green and turn into a prepared 7-inch tin. Bake in a moderate oven for approximately 50–60 minutes (4, C or 350°).

When cold, finish the top and sides of the cake with American icing, decorating quickly and casually with pieces of sliced glacé pineapple, half cherries and silver balls.

ALMOND DUCHESS CAKE

A rich Madeira mixture forms the basis of this excellent cake, while a thin layer of marzipan baked in the centre makes it even more interesting to eat.

6 oz butter or margarine *6 oz flour*
6 oz castor sugar *½ teaspoon baking powder*
3 eggs *a little almond and vanilla essence*

Marzipan :

3 oz ground almonds *1½ oz icing sugar*
1½ oz castor sugar *egg to bind*
a few flaked almonds to sprinkle over the top of the cake

Begin by preparing a 7-inch cake tin by lining it with paper.

Next prepare the marzipan. Put the ground almonds and castor sugar into a bowl. Sieve in the icing sugar and mix all to a stiff paste with egg. Turn on to a sugared board and roll into a circle of the same size as the cake tin.

Now prepare the actual cake mixture. Cream the butter (or margarine) and sugar thoroughly and gradually beat in the whisked eggs. Add the almond and vanilla essences and lightly beat in the flour and baking powder. Spread half the mixture in the bottom of the cake tin. Place the layer of marzipan on top, pressing it home with the fingers. Cover with the remainder of the mixture and sprinkle with flaked almonds. Bake at 4, C, or 350° for 1¼–1½ hours.

A PLEASING ORANGE CAKE

6 oz margarine *6 oz flour*
6 oz castor sugar *½ teaspoon baking powder*
3 eggs *the rind and juice of 1 orange*

Icing :

4 oz icing sugar
boiling orange juice to mix to a spreading consistency

Decoration :

finely-chopped orange peel

Cream the margarine and sugar thoroughly. Add the grated orange rind and gradually beat in the whisked eggs and the orange juice. With the last of these, start adding the flour and baking powder. Bake in a 7-inch cake tin at 350°, 4 or C for approximately ³/₄ hour.

When cold, spread the top with the orange icing and decorate round the edge with finely-chopped peel. Alternately, the top of the cake may be spread with marmalade, scattered with pieces of peel and cherry and the orange-flavoured icing used to veil all.

COCONUT MACAROON CAKE

8 oz margarine
8 oz castor sugar
4 eggs and 1 yolk of egg
8 oz flour

¹/₂ teaspoon baking powder
1 oz ground almonds
1 oz fine coconut
vanilla essence

Coconut macaroon mixture :

1 white of egg
3 oz castor sugar
¹/₂ oz fine coconut
a few flaked almonds to sprinkle over the top of the cake

1 oz ground almonds
vanilla essence

Cream the margarine and sugar thoroughly and gradually beat in the whisked eggs and the vanilla essence. With the last of the egg add the remaining dry ingredients. Turn the mixture into a prepared 8-inch cake tin.

Now prepare the coconut macaroon mixture. Lightly whisk the white of egg and fold in the other ingredients. Spread over the top of the cake mixture already in the tin. Sprinkle with flaked almonds and bake at 4, C or 350° for approximately 1³/₄ hours.

GATEAU PAIN de GENES

This is a strange name for a cake, since translated literally it means "uneasy bread." The title is perhaps justified however, as the cake tends to be a "sinker" and to have a moist line running across the centre. Do not let this sorry description prevent you trying the recipe, for the mixture makes rich and delicious eating.

4 oz butter	*1½ oz flour*
5 oz castor sugar	*a small glass of kirsch*
3½ oz ground almonds	*or sherry*
3 eggs	

Cream the butter and sugar thoroughly. Then work in the ground almonds and again beat thoroughly. Next, add the whisked eggs gradually and lastly the flour and flavouring. Turn into a 7-inch cake tin previously lined with paper and bake in a very moderate oven for approximately 40 minutes. Suggested oven temperatures being 4, C or 350°.

MARBLE SPICE CAKE

8 oz margarine	*8 oz flour*
8 oz castor sugar	*½ teaspoon baking powder*
½ teaspoon vanilla essence	*2 oz chopped walnuts*
4 eggs	*¾ teaspoon ground cinnamon*
a little milk as necessary	*¼ teaspoon ground cloves*
	¼ teaspoon ground nutmeg

Filling :

  approximately 4 oz marshmallows

Coffee fudge icing .

8 oz granulated sugar	*1 dessertspoon coffee essence*
2 oz margarine	*1 gill evaporated milk*

Decoration : a few walnuts.

Cream the margarine and sugar together. Flavour with the vanilla essence and gradually beat in the lightly-whisked eggs. With the last of the egg beat in the flour and baking powder. Add a little milk as necessary if the mixture is too stiff.

Now divide the mixture in two and, to one half, add the chopped walnuts. To the other half add the spices. Put these two mixtures spoonful about into a lined 8-inch cake tin. Then bake in a moderate oven for 1½–1¾ hours. Suggested oven temperatures being 4, C or 350°.

When cold, split and cover the bottom half of the cake with marshmallow sweets cut in two. Put under a gently-heated grill to melt, then place the other half of the cake on top.

Now prepare the coffee fudge icing. Put the ingredients for the icing into a strong saucepan, and stir over a gentle heat until the sugar is dissolved. Then bring to the boil, stirring all the time and boil until a little, when tested in cold water, will give a soft ball. Remove from the heat and beat until beginning to thicken; then use quickly to coat the cake. Decorate with walnuts.

CARAMEL NUT CAKE

Caramel:

⅓ cup soft brown sugar	3 tablespoons hot water

Cake mixture:

6 oz margarine	1½ teaspoons baking powder
10 oz castor sugar	½ teaspoon salt
½ teaspoon vanilla essence	1¼ cups milk
3 eggs	½ cup chopped walnuts
12 oz flour	

Fudge icing:

2 teacups soft brown sugar	1 oz margarine
½ cup milk	½ teaspoon vanilla essence

Begin by preparing the caramel. Put the soft brown sugar into a small, strong saucepan and heat gently until liquid and brown. Stir in the hot water adding it gradually and, when dissolved, put aside to cool.

Meanwhile prepare the cake mixture. Cream the margarine and the sugar together. Flavour with the vanilla essence and gradually beat in the caramel and the whisked eggs. Then add the flour, baking powder and salt alternately with the milk. Lastly stir in the chopped walnuts. Turn the mixture into a lined 8-inch cake tin. Bake in a moderate oven for approximately 1½ hours. Suggested temperatures being 4, C or 350°.

When cold prepare the icing. Put the sugar, milk and margarine into a medium-sized saucepan and heat gently until the sugar is dissolved. Then bring to the boil and, stirring all the time, boil until a little, when tested in cold water, will form a soft ball. Remove from the heat. Add the vanilla essence and beat until it begins to thicken; then use quickly to ice the cake. Decorate by sprinkling with chopped walnuts.

These next three cakes are not plain enough to be called bread, nor rich enough to be really and truly cake, but are good to eat all the same. Serve, generously spread with butter.

A SODA CAKE

1 lb flour	6 oz demerara sugar
1 teaspoon salt	4 oz sultanas or raisins
1 teaspoon baking soda	2 oz peel
a grating of nutmeg	2 eggs
6 oz margarine	approx ½ pint milk

Sieve the flour, salt and baking soda together. Grate in a little nutmeg; cut and rub in the margarine. Add the demerara sugar and the fruit and mix all to a soft dough with the beaten egg and milk. Turn into an 8-inch cake tin and bake at 5, D or 375° for 1½–2 hours.

LUNCHEON CAKE

1 lb flour	4 oz sultanas
1 teaspoon salt	4 oz currants
2 teaspoons baking powder	2 oz candied peel
2 teaspoons mixed spice	1 dessertspoon treacle
6 oz margarine	2 eggs
6 oz sugar	approx ½ pint milk

Sieve the flour, salt, baking powder and spice into a bowl. Cut and rub in the margarine. Add the fruit and sugar. Then mix to a soft consistency with the eggs, treacle and milk. Turn into an 8-inch cake tin and bake in a fairly hot oven for approximately 1½ hours. Suggested oven temperatures being 5, D or 375°.

CINNAMON TEA CAKE

8 oz flour	*3 oz castor sugar*
½ teaspoon salt	*1 large egg*
1½ teaspoon baking powder	*¼ pint milk*
3 oz margarine	

Cinnamon crumble:

1 oz flour	*½ teaspoon ground cinnamon*
2 oz castor sugar	*1½ oz margarine*

Sieve the 8 oz flour, salt and baking powder into a bowl. Cut and rub in the margarine and add the sugar. Mix all to a soft batter using the beaten egg and milk. Turn into an 8-inch cake tin.

Next prepare the cinnamon mixture. Put the flour, sugar and cinnamon in a bowl and crumb the margarine through. Sprinkle over the plain mixture in the tin and bake at 5, D or 375° for 35–40 minutes.

CHERRY CAKE

Cherry cake is not an easy one to make well, for all too often the fruit falls to the bottom. However, should this happen, take comfort in the fact that the bottom layer tastes truly delicious.

To be more matter of fact however, there are many theories on how to make the cherries obey the rules:—some cooks use a recipe in which there is a big proportion of flour compared with the butter, sugar and eggs, others wash the cherries in hot water to remove the syrup and so make them lighter, while often they are tossed in ground almonds, again with the idea of giving them buoyancy. I do not feel happy that these suggestions are really worthwhile, in that they do not always result in a cake which tastes well. However, the following recipe is excellent to eat and nearly foolproof to make.

8 oz butter

8 oz castor sugar

4 eggs

8 oz flour

1/2 teaspoon baking powder

4 oz ground almonds

8 oz glacé cherries, quartered

2 oz citron peel, chopped

the rind and juice of 1 lemon

Cream the butter and sugar thoroughly, then beat in the lightly-whisked eggs and with the last of the egg add the flour and baking powder. Meanwhile have the cherries and citron peel mixed through the ground almonds and add to the cake batter, together with the lemon rind and juice. Turn into a prepared 8-inch cake tin and bake in a moderate oven (4, C or 350°) for approximately 2 hours.

A RICH CHERRY CAKE
ridiculously rich, but a lovely colour when cut

There are so many cherries that it is hardly possible for them to fall.

4 oz butter

4 oz castor sugar

2 eggs

4 oz flour

the rind and juice of 1 lemon

1/4 teaspoon baking powder

2 oz ground almonds

2 oz citron peel

2 lb glacé cherries

Almond paste for the centre of the cake :

3 oz ground almonds

1 1/2 oz castor sugar

1 1/2 oz icing sugar

a little beaten egg to bind

Begin by lining an 8-inch cake tin with paper.

Next prepare the almond paste. Put the ground almonds and castor sugar into a bowl. Sieve in the icing sugar and mix all to a stiff paste with egg. Turn on to a sugared board and roll into a circle of the same size as the cake tin.

Now prepare the actual cake mixture. Cream the butter and sugar thoroughly and gradually beat in the whisked eggs and the rind and juice of a lemon. With the last of the egg add the flour and baking powder. Finally stir in the ground almonds, chopped citron peel and the whole glacé cherries.

Spread half this mixture in the bottom of the cake tin. Place the layer of almond paste on top, pressing it home with the fingers. Cover with the remainder of the cherry mixture. Bake in a moderately-heated oven for $2\frac{1}{2}$–3 hours. Suggested oven temperatures being 2, B or 325°–300°.

If wished, this cake may be iced with white water icing before use.

It is best stored some days before cutting.

A RICH FRUIT CAKE
extravagant and luscious—a cake for the special occasion

$\frac{1}{2}$ lb sultanas	$\frac{1}{2}$ lb glacé pineapple
3 tablespoons brandy	2 oz preserved ginger
$\frac{1}{2}$ lb butter	2 oz citron peel
$\frac{1}{2}$ lb castor sugar	3 oz angelica
4 eggs	2 oz walnuts
$\frac{1}{2}$ lb flour	the grated rind and juice of 1 lemon
$\frac{1}{2}$ lb glacé cherries	

Steep the sultanas in the brandy overnight.

Next day cream the butter and sugar thoroughly and gradually beat in the eggs; then with the last of the egg, add the flour. Meanwhile have the various fruits roughly chopped; if wished keeping back some of the nicer pieces to decorate the top of the cake. Add the fruit to the cake batter and turn into a prepared 8-inch cake tin. Decorate, if you fancy, with walnuts and thin slices of citron peel. Bake in a moderate oven (2, B or 325°–300°) for approximately $2\frac{1}{2}$ hours.

AN AMERICAN FRUIT CAKE

3 cups fine coconut	1 cup glacé cherries
1 cup chopped dates	1 cup mixed fruits, e. g. citron
1 cup chopped walnuts	peel and ginger
1 cup raisins	$1\frac{1}{2}$ cups sweetened condensed milk
1 cup dried, chopped apricots	a little vanilla

Mix all the ingredients together in a bowl. Then pack into an 8-inch cake tin which has been lined with greased paper. Decorate the top of the cake with some of the cherries, thin slices of peel and half walnuts. Bake in a slow oven for 1½–2 hours. Suggested oven temperatures being 1, A or 300°

When cold, wrap in greaseproof paper and store for some weeks to ripen before cutting.

A RICH PLUM CAKE
an eccentric recipe but one which is, nevertheless, well worth trying

½ lb butter	½ lb chopped almonds
½ lb soft brown sugar	1 lb raisins
2 oz dark chocolate	1 lb sultanas
½ lb flour	1 lb currants
½ teaspoon ground cinnamon	¾ lb mixed candied peel
½ teaspoon mixed spice	1 teaspoon lemon juice
½ teaspoon ground nutmeg	1 small tin strawberries
6 eggs	sherry, whisky or rum to soak the
½ lb glacé cherries	cake when baked

Cream the butter and sugar thoroughly and beat in the melted chocolate.

Now sieve the flour and the spices and divide into three parts. Use these as follows:— Add the first part to the creamed mixture together with the egg yolks. Beat all thoroughly. Add the second part together with the stiffly-beaten egg whites. Add the third part with the prepared fruit. Lastly add the drained strawberries and lemon juice.

Turn the mixture into a prepared 8–9-inch tin and bake in a very moderate oven for 2½–3 hours (2–3, B or 325°–300°).

When cooked, baste with 3–4 tablespoons sherry, whisky or rum.

TRADITIONAL CAKES

SIMNEL CAKE

SIMNEL Cake is of ancient origin and reaches us in the 20th century surrounded by much myth and legend. So much so that it is difficult to choose the truth from the fable. It is certain, however, that the cake has been known and made over a very long period and its name is accounted by many to have been derived from a Latin word "simila" meaning fine flour. It has long been associated with Mothering Sunday which came as a break in the midst of the austerities of Lent. Originally Mothering Sunday was a day to honour the Mother Church at Jerusalem and it is believed that the traditional marzipan balls which are used in the decoration of the Simnel cake represent the apostles who founded the original church.

Another entertaining, but more doubtful, story connected with Simnel cakes is that the father of Lambeth Simnel, the well known Pretender in the reign of Henry VII was a baker and the first maker of Simnels and that in consequence of the celebrity he gained through his son, his cakes were honoured with his name.

A further charming tale of how the name Simnel originated is told in Shropshire. It concerns an old couple called Simon and Nell who were looking forward to a visit from their family on Mothering Sunday. They wished to make a special cake for the occasion and had, as materials, ingredients left over from their Christmas pudding and some pastry. These they decided to use but, regrettably, they had a quarrel over the way in which the cake should be cooked. Simon said it should be boiled; Nell thought it should be baked. They argued fiercely to the point of Nell throwing a stool at her husband. However they finally reached a happy solution and the cake was both boiled *and* baked. The broken stool was used as fuel for the fire and, when the cake was proudly presented to the family, they pronounced it good and christened it Simnel cake. Be that as it may, it is interesting to note that in Devizes in Wiltshire it is traditional to both boil and bake this type of cake.

The modern version. Nowadays the custom of making Simnel cake for Mothering Sunday seems to have lapsed and we tend to think of it as a cake for Easter. Certainly when the family is on holiday it is essential to have a good cutting cake to hand and Simnel cake seems ideal. It is luscious, spicy, rich and good to eat, with its double layer

FIG. 19. *Simnel Cake.*
Iced with royal icing in addition to the layer of almond paste. The traditional
style of decoration is combined with the modern

of almond paste; and many claim they find it even more delicious than a Christmas cake.
Finally, those who are artistic and ingenious can decorate it most attractively and in
keeping with the season.

The following recipe will make a cake of average size and is suitable for baking
in an 8-inch cake tin.

6 oz butter or margarine	*2 teaspoons mixed spice*
6 oz castor sugar	*8 oz sultanas*
4 eggs	*8 oz rāisins*
6 oz flour	*2 oz candied peel*
½ teaspoon baking powder	

168

FIG. 20. *Simnel Cake.*
Decorated with an Easter bird contrived from two marshmallow sweets

Almond paste made from 6 oz ground almonds is required for the layer in the centre of the cake, and a second quantity made from 8 oz ground almonds is required to finish the cake. The recipe for this is given later.

When setting out to mix a Simnel cake try to have plenty of time for the work in hand. Actually when one thinks about it, two mixtures must be prepared, before it can be put in the oven and so leisure is necessary if one is to enjoy making the cake.

Begin by cleaning the fruit and lining an 8-inch round cake tin.

Next prepare the almond paste, which is to be cooked in the centre of the cake, and roll it to the exact dimensions of the cake tin.

Then, having completed these preliminaries, prepare the actual cake mixture, as follows. Cream the butter and sugar thoroughly. Add the beaten eggs alternately with

169

FIG. 21. *Simnel Cake.*
Decorated with lush crystallised peaches interspaced between the balls of toasted marzipan

the flour, and lastly stir in the fruit, spice and baking powder. Put half the mixture into the cake tin, lay the almond paste on top, press into position and cover with the remainder of the cake mixture. Bake in a moderately-heated oven until the cake is firm to the touch. It will require approximately $2\frac{1}{2}$ hours. Suggested oven temperatures being 2–3, B or 325°–300°.

Icing the cake. It is customary to ice the Simnel cake with a layer of almond icing and to decorate it with balls of the icing arranged round the edge of the cake. Any further decoration usually takes the form of fluffy chickens, miniature Easter eggs or even glacé fruits.

This is what you do. Make up the second amount of almond paste and keep back about one-third to use for decoration. Roll the remainder to a round the size of the

FIG. 22. *Simnel Cake.*
Decorated with a rope of toasted marzipan instead of the marzipan balls.
The centre of the cake is piled with roughly chopped crystallised fruits

cake. Brush with egg and invert the cake on to the paste. Press well together and neaten the edges with a knife. Turn right side up and the cake is ready for decoration.

The finishing touches. First of all a pleasant effect may be obtained by pressing the almond paste with a wire cake cooler. You will find this marks it neatly into little squares. Then pinch round the edge as you would a round of shortbread and decorate with balls of marzipan, stuck in position with egg. These are usually placed so as to form a circle but I sometimes arrange them horse-shoe fashion according to the final decoration. Brush the balls with more egg and toast a pretty golden colour in a hot oven. It is important to have the oven really hot for this purpose otherwise it is necessary to leave the cake in over long and, of course, this will dry it out. The almond paste should brown inside 5 minutes if the temperature is correct.

171

Alternatively the balls of almond paste may be browned separately before putting on the cake.

A rich and colourful decoration. The centre now remains to be decorated and here the artist has great opportunity.

A favourite method of mine is to pile neatly cut glacé fruits in the centre of the cake. Suggested fruit would include a mixture of cherries, pineapple, and angelica, while it is well to remember that cherries can be obtained in shades of yellow and green as well as red. In order to hold them in position, a little water icing should be spread over the centre part of the cake and, while it is still moist, the fruit piled on top in such a way as to completely hide the icing.

Yet another way to use cherries with effect is to interspace them between the balls of almond paste. If wished they may be tossed in granulated sugar, dried in the oven to give a candied effect and, finally, a diamond of angelica inserted in the cavity left by the cherry stone. If wished, the centre of this cake may be left plain, but it is more attractive if sprinkled with toasted shredded almonds held in position by a brushing of white of egg. Finally dust the almonds lightly with icing sugar.

These decorations, besides giving the cake a rich and colourful appearance, are very easy to copy, and a professional finish is assured.

A Decoration to please the family. If there are children in the house a cake planned to please them is required. Fluffy chickens or miniature Easter eggs are often used, while a simple and truly effective decoration can be made from a broken egg shell, coloured prettily, arranged on top of the cake with an Easter chicken set in the middle. It should look as if it has just arrived!

Those who are skilful at modelling will doubtless enjoy making chickens, ducks and rabbits from coloured marzipan. Make some tiny spring flowers too, to indicate a proper lightness of heart.

ALMOND PASTE

8 oz ground almonds
4 oz castor sugar
4 oz sieved icing sugar

almond essence
beaten egg to mix

Mix the ground almonds with the two varieties of sugar and flavour with almond essence. Mix to a stiff paste with beaten egg.

172

BURY SIMNEL

Bury, in Lancashire, is famous for an ancient form of Simnel bread which was made by its bakers and sold in the shops on Mothering Sunday. Since it was against the law to buy and sell on the Sabbath, much friction ensued, but the bread was so popular that the custom persisted somewhat modified by the regulation that no shopping should take place during a church service.

This traditional Bury Simnel is quite unlike the usually accepted version of a Simnel cake and is more in the nature of a very fruity bread. It is, nevertheless, well worth making.

5 oz flour	*¼ grated nutmeg*
1 oz margarine	*8 oz currants*
1 oz lard	*1 oz candied peel*
½ teaspoon baking powder	*1 egg*
3 oz castor sugar	*a little milk if necessary*
½ teaspoon ground cinnamon	

whole blanched almonds or walnuts, cherries and thinly-sliced citron peel to decorate

Rub the two fats into the flour and then add the other dry ingredients mixing well. Beat the egg and use to mix all to a very stiff dough, adding a small quantity of milk in addition if necessary. Form into a round flat cake on a greased baking tray, rather like a tea-cake in shape. Decorate with the nuts, cherries and peel and bake for about 30 minutes in an oven set at 6, E or 400°.

A FAVOURITE FROM SCOTLAND

Scots Currant Bun, or Black Bun, as it is also called, is a festive cake intended for eating at Hogmanay. It consists of a very rich fruit mixture baked in a casing of short crust pastry. It keeps well and is a splendid cake to make as a standby for cutting.

SCOTS CURRANT BUN

The pastry:

6 oz flour

$3\frac{1}{2}$ oz margarine

1 teaspoon castor sugar

a pinch of salt

cold water to mix

The bun mixture:

$1\frac{1}{2}$ lb currants

$\frac{1}{4}$ lb large raisins

$\frac{1}{4}$ lb candied peel

$\frac{1}{4}$ lb almonds

$\frac{1}{4}$ lb sugar

6 oz flour

$\frac{1}{4}$ oz ground allspice

$\frac{1}{4}$ oz ground ginger

$\frac{1}{4}$ oz ground cinnamon

$\frac{1}{4}$ teaspoon pepper

$\frac{1}{2}$ teaspoon cream of tartar

$\frac{1}{2}$ teaspoon baking soda

1 gill milk

Making the pastry casing: Make the pastry by rubbing the margarine into the dry ingredients and mix to a stiff dough with cold water. Divide into three pieces: these are for lining the top, bottom and sides of the cake tin respectively. The cake tin should be greased but it is not necessary to line it with paper. Commence by rolling one piece into a long thin strip for the sides of an 8-inch cake tin. The necessary measurements can be conveniently taken with a piece of string. Use this strip to line the sides, pressing out the join with the fingers. Next roll out the two remaining pieces of pastry thinly and cut two circles for the top and bottom of the bun. Damp the bottom edge of the pastry already lining the sides of the tin and press the bottom circle into position. The pastry casing is now ready for filling.

Making the currant bun mixture. As with any rich fruit mixture it is wisest to spread the actual making of the cake over two days. On the first day all the preparation of the fruit is completed. Currants are often very dirty and will require washing, while the raisins may require both washing and stoning. Wash the fruit in tepid water and, if very dry and hard, allow it perhaps 15–20 minutes to soak and swell. Then pick over carefully and spread out to dry in a warm place. The almonds are prepared by shredding. They are not usually blanched for this cake since the skin helps to keep the colour of the mixture dark. Shred the candied peel also.

Next day, put the fruit, nuts, peel, flour, sugar, cream of tartar, baking soda and spices into a large basin. Add the milk and stir until thoroughly combined. The mixture when ready should be moist but not damp. It is then ready to be pressed into the lined tin. Make the surface flat and smooth. Turn in ¼-inch of the pastry lining the sides, damp and place the circle of pastry for the top in position. Make all secure and neat. Prick well with a fork and brush with beaten egg.

The baking. Scots Currant Bun is very rich, like a plum cake, and therefore the baking of it is somewhat similar. It should be placed in the middle of a very moderately-heated oven and baked slowly for approximately 3½ hours. Suggested temperatures being either 2–3, B or 325°–300°.

THE CHRISTMAS CAKE

The Christmas Cake is undoubtedly the cake of the year and housewives give its making great thought and care, so that the result is as nearly perfect as possible. The actual recipe used is often an old family one, handed down from mother to daughter. So it is in my own family, and the recipe which follows has stood the test of many years.

Achieving perfection. The Christmas cake should be baked well in advance, perhaps during November, since it mellows and improves with keeping. Indeed, some keen bakers like to make it in the late summer and store it away, wrapped in a generous thickness of greaseproof paper with, perhaps, a cooking apple in the cake tin to keep it company.

A well-baked cake is one which is moist to the touch and to eat. In this connection the actual baking is of the utmost importance and it is well to remember that more cakes are spoiled by being over-baked than the reverse. Exact oven temperatures are given later with the time for baking but these at best are only approximate. In the long run good judgment is necessary, to know just when the cake is ready. To pierce the cake with a skewer is a well-known test but experienced bakers can always tell by feeling the centre with their fingers. When ready, it should feel firm to the touch.

A well-baked plum cake is also one which is perfectly flat, so that it may be iced without trimming, and it goes without saying that it should be evenly browned.

½ lb butter	¼ lb glacé cherries
½ lb Barbados sugar	2 oz ground almonds
4–5 eggs	1 teaspoon ground ginger

½ lb flour	½ teaspoon ground allspice
1 lb currants	½ teaspoon ground cinnamon
½ lb sultanas	½ teaspoon ground cloves
¼ lb raisins	½ teaspoon ground corriander
¼ lb candied peel	½ gill brandy or whisky if wished

It is better to divide the making of the Christmas Cake over a period of two days, as follows:—

On the first day all tedious preparation should be undertaken; fruit should be carefully washed, picked over and dried, cherries and peel chopped and the cake tin lined with two thicknesses of paper. Incidentally, it is unnecessary to grease the paper.

On the second day the actual mixing and baking can be carried out easily. Start by creaming the butter and sugar until light and soft. Then gradually beat in the eggs and flour alternately. The eggs may be dropped in one at a time, whole. Lastly, add the fruit and spices. Turn into the prepared cake tin and slightly hollow out the centre, since this helps to ensure a flat cake when baked.

Baking hints: The above quantity may be baked in an 8-inch cake tin, or divided between two 7-inch tins. The former will require approximately 3 hours in the oven and the latter 2–2½ hours.

Exact oven temperatures are as follows: electric ovens—325°–300°, placing the cake in the centre of the oven; gas ovens—2–3 or B, placing the cake low in the oven.

When the cake is baked, while it is still hot and in the tin, it should be lightly basted with the spirits. This is optional, of course, but it undoubtedly improves the flavour, texture and keeping qualities of the cake. When cold, wrap the cake in greaseproof paper and store in an airtight tin for icing later.

ICING THE CHRISTMAS CAKE

Decorating the Christmas cake is a fascinating task and it is worth giving it time and patience so that the result is a real triumph. On this score, therefore, it is important to complete the work before the final Christmas rush begins.

The cake may be iced with almond paste only and decorated with glacé fruit or with figures, flowers, fruit or holly fashioned in marzipan. Alternatively, the marzipan may be covered with a white icing before it is decorated.

The preparation of the cake. To make a good job of the icing, the cake should be perfectly level on top. If necessary, it is really worth cutting a little away to correct any unevenness.

THE ALMOND PASTE

For covering the top of a 7-inch cake, half a pound of almond paste is sufficient and, if the sides are to be iced as well, then three-quarters of a pound of ground almonds should be used. These quantities will give a $\frac{1}{2}$-inch layer of icing over the cake.

$\frac{1}{2}$ lb ground almonds	1 dessertspoon sherry
4 oz castor sugar	a little almond and vanilla essence
4 oz sieved icing sugar	egg to bind

Mix the ground almonds and the two sugars together. Add the flavourings and mix to a stiff paste with lightly-beaten egg.

It is worth noting, if white icing is also being made, that the whites of egg will be required for it and the yolks may be used in the mixing of the almond paste.

TO ALMOND ICE THE TOP OF A CAKE

Dust the pastry board with sugar. Knead and roll the paste to the exact size of the cake. Brush with beaten egg and invert the cake on to the icing. Press firmly together and neaten the edge with a knife, keeping the cake level. Turn the cake right-side up and decorate as you please.

In the first place the surface of the marzipan may be left quite plain or finished in some simple way. The former is more suitable if the marzipan has been put on with great neatness and if the further decoration is trim and tailored. Otherwise the surface may be roughened with a fork or marked, trellis fashion, by pressing a cooling wire into the soft icing and then pinching the edge as in making shortbread.

DECORATIONS

Decorations follow and will vary, of course, according to the time available and the ability of the cook to model in marzipan. It is worth remembering, however, that often the simplest decorations are the most pleasing.

Colourful and charming effects can quickly be obtained by using glacé fruits such as cherries, angelica and pineapple. The cherries are made more interesting for this purpose if they are first tossed in granulated sugar and dried in a warm oven. Sometimes, too, I pipe them spiral fashion with a little royal icing and find this gives a quick and gay result.

MODELLING IN MARZIPAN

The best marzipan for modelling is one which is made using only icing sugar and which is mixed with white of egg. This will have a fine texture and light colour and various colourings can then be kneaded into it as required.

HOLLY AND MISTLETOE are probably the most generally useful of all marzipan decorations and the method I use to fashion them is as follows.

First of all cut a template of a holly and mistletoe leaf, and use these as guides to cut them from thinly-rolled, coloured marzipan. I like to have the marzipan shaded in two tones of green for holly, the shading indicating the central vein of the leaf. Use a fine, sharp penknife as a tool for cutting the marzipan cleanly.

Berries are easy to make using natural coloured marzipan for the mistletoe, while the red, holly berries are more realistic if the calyx is indicated with a tiny clipping from a clove.

I usually allow these decorations to harden before placing them on the cake and then it is possible to get a raised effect easily.

MAKING VIOLETS. A bunch of violets makes a most attractive decoration on a Christmas cake and is quite easy to do. Usually four leaves are required and these are made from thinly-rolled green marzipan cut with a small plain cutter. They should be arranged roughly in the form of a cross and slightly raised on the outer side. Next come the flowers and each is made using two circles of violet marzipan. These should be as thin as possible, especially at the edge, and I use an éclair pipe to cut them. Roll the first circle between the fingers and thumb to obtain the centre of the flower, touching the edges with the finger to give it a pretty curl. Arrange the second circle, petal fashion, around the first and mass these violets in the centre of the leaves.

Stems are easy and the whole effect most realistic.

FIGURES in marzipan can be most fascinating in clever hands and can range from a cute little snowman to the heavenly angels, complete with carol music.

Marshmallow sweets and cocktail sticks can also be useful, in this connection, for making funny birds and animals.

TO ALMOND PASTE THE ENTIRE CAKE

If the cake is to be finished with a white icing it is best to cover it first with almond paste. This will prevent the crumb of the cake getting into the icing while it is being put on and also prevent the natural juices of the cake seeping through in the course of time.

First, divide the piece of almond paste in two. Roll one half into a long narrow strip. This is for the sides of the cake and the necessary length and width can easily be measured by using a piece of string. Brush the strip with egg and roll the cake along it, pressing gently to make the marzipan stick. Cover the top of the cake with the second piece of almond paste as directed previously.

Finally the white icing:—

YOUR CHOICE

There are two varieties of white icing commonly used on a Christmas cake—royal icing and mountain, or American, icing. Of these the royal icing is the simpler to make but many people find the mountain icing nicer to eat. Instructions for making both follow and beginners are recommended to try the first icing. Experienced cooks should certainly make the second variety for, while it is a little tricky to make, it is extremely good and if the instructions are accurately followed it should be successful.

ROYAL ICING

This icing is easy to make and is excellent for coating the cake and piping. For a simple decoration it is sometimes roughened up, to make it like a snow scene, and further decorated with small figures, little Christmas trees and so on.

³⁄₄ lb icing sugar
enough white of egg to give a stiff result
a squeeze of lemon juice

179

Sieve the icing sugar using a hair or nylon sieve. Put it in a bowl, add the lemon juice and sufficient lightly-beaten white of egg to give a stiff mixture. Beat thoroughly, and use as required.

While the actual icing is in progress it is wise to keep the bowl of mixture covered with a damp cloth, otherwise it begins to set on the surface and so might cause lumpiness.

MOUNTAIN ICING

The instructions should be followed carefully, since this icing is undoubtedly tricky to make and quick and accurate decisions are necessary in judging when the icing has reached the correct consistency for putting on the cake. At this stage it can set very quickly, so speed is essential.

1 lb granulated sugar	*a pinch of cream of tartar*
1 gill water	*2 whites of egg*

Put the water and sugar into a strong saucepan, place over a gentle heat and stir until the sugar is dissolved. Then stir in the pinch of cream of tartar and bring to the boil. Boil briskly without stirring until a little, when tested in cold water, will give a "soft ball" or until 240° is reached. Meanwhile ask an assistant to put the two whites in a large bowl and to whisk them until stiff. Once the syrup is ready, gently pour it on to the whites, beating all the time. Continue whisking until the mixture thickens and shows signs of holding its shape. Working quickly, spread the icing over the cake, leaving the surface rough like a snow scene.

THE DECORATION

The decoration should be put in position immediately and you will find that it is easy to give this type of cake a festive appearance. Little snow-men can be bought and used effectively, while a gay result may be obtained by sticking bows into the icing at the angle between the cake and the cake board. My favourite material for making these bows is crimson cellophane, for its transparency and glisten makes it specially attractive.

Again those who can model in marzipan will enjoy themselves and many of the decorations suggested earlier look equally pretty on the white icing.

Simple suggestions include a cake bedecked with red Christmas stars cut from thin red marzipan and in various sizes and scattered at random over the surface. Or sprigs of holly and mistletoe here and there over the top and sides. This last decoration reminds me to mention that "white icing" need not always be white and that pale green or peach shades can often be very pretty looking, although, in planning any decoration for a Christmas cake, it is wise to lay stress on the seasonable colours of red and green.

❧   ❧   ❧

WEDDING CAKE

A wedding cake is the most important cake of all and often a bride will take great pleasure in making it herself. There is tremendous satisfaction to be gained from such a task, while the quality of the ingredients can be guaranteed and yet the cost of this expensive cake kept to a minimum. Naturally it is easier to bake a good cake than it is to ice it in a style worthy of the occasion and so the home-made cake is often handed over to an expert for icing and decorating later.

The recipe used for a wedding cake is one for a rich plum-cake mixture. The quantities will naturally depend on the size of the cake and the number of tiers, and most home bakers find they are a little baffled as to the correct decision in this matter. However, when faced with such a problem, proceed as follows and you can be confident of the results:—

In the first place always use a recipe for a rich plum cake with which you are familiar and happy. This will probably be the mixture favoured for the Christmas cake. It follows that the size of the cake tin will be known exactly and, using water, it is easy to find the volume of the cake. From this it is a simple matter to find the volume of the tins to be used for the wedding cake and so to calculate the quantities of cake mixture necessary.

A wedding cake may consist of one, two or three tiers and if it is to have good proportions it is important that the dimensions of the tiers should be carefully chosen. Suitable sizes are a 12-inch cake for the base, an 8–8½-inch one for the middle and a 6-inch cake for the top.

To bake these cakes in an ordinary domestic oven needs care, but can be done. It is, of course, the large cake which is the difficulty since the sides of the cake come rather near to the source of heat. It is therefore necessary to line the tin with 3–4 thicknesses of paper and, in addition, to tie a stout band of newspaper round the outside of the large tin. As with other rich cakes, it is not necessary to grease the paper, since the cake will not stick and the fat on the paper would cause the crust to darken unnecessarily.

The cake should be placed low in the oven and it is recommended that the large cake be baked by itself and the two smaller cakes later. If wished, the mixture for all three cakes can be made at once, for it will not take any harm if the baking is delayed even until the next day. Incidentally, if a mixing machine is not available, it is better and easier to cream the butter and sugar using the hand instead of a wooden spoon. When the cakes are set and coloured it is wise to cover them with a double sheet of paper.

Oven temperatures are, of course, the same as for a Christmas cake, that is 2, B or 300°. A 12-inch cake will require approximately $4\frac{1}{2}$ hours; an 8-inch cake $3-3\frac{1}{2}$ hours and a 6 inch cake $2-2\frac{1}{2}$ hours. As always be careful not to over-bake.

When cooked, remove from the oven and baste with brandy or other spirits, as wished. Allow to cool in the tin and, next day, wrap in generous layers of greaseproof paper for storing. Preferably, the cakes should be stored in air-tight tins, but with the large cake this is sometimes a problem. Ingenuity will come to your aid however and, perhaps, a preserving pan or boiler will serve the purpose instead of a tin.

A wedding cake is all the better for having time to mature and it is not too long to have it baked three months before it is required. At the end of two months the cakes should be covered with a layer of almond icing and this given a little time to dry out before being coated with royal icing. If this is not done there is a tendency for the oil from the almonds to discolour it.

PLATE 3. *Christmas Cake*. To please the children. This cake was baked in a 12 inch cake tin with a smaller tin set in the centre to form a large ring

PLATE 4. *Christmas Cake.* Little choir boys modelled in marzipan be-deck this cake

PLATE 5. *Christmas Cake* in which citron peel and piped cherries have been used to give an effective, yet simple, decoration

FACTS AND FIGURES

HANDY MEASURES

WHILE, for exact work, the use of scales always gives the most satisfactory results when baking, it is often advantageous to have a knowledge of some handy ways of measuring for use when speed is more important than accuracy or when no scales are available, as occasionally happens. In these circumstances the following table of homely measures will be found helpful:—

1 oz flour = 1 fully rounded tablespoonful
1 oz castor, granulated or demerara sugar = 1 rounded tablespoonful
2 oz golden syrup, or treacle = 1 rounded tablespoonful
1 oz coconut = 1 rounded tablespoonful
1 oz dried fruit = 1 rounded tablespoonful

An 8 oz block of margarine can easily be cut into 4 oz, 2 oz, and 1 oz pieces as required, while butter and cooking fats can be measured in a similar way.

1 teacupful of liquid = fully 1 gill
1 breakfast-cupful of liquid = fully ½ pint
1 tumblerful of liquid = approximately ½ pint

These measurements are of course only approximate, for a great deal can depend on the care with which the individual does the measuring.

COINS AS A SUBSTITUTE FOR WEIGHTS

Sometimes scales are available but the small weights are easily lost and, if this is the problem, it useful to know that:—

3 pennies = 1 oz
1 penny and 1 halfpenny = ½ oz
1 halfpenny and 1 silver 3d piece = ¼ oz

BRITISH AND AMERICAN MEASURES

While we, in Britain, generally work with scales and weigh ingredients, across the Atlantic standard measuring cups and spoons are used instead. This can lead to errors, when recipes are being converted from one system to the other, since it is not always realised that British and American spoons are of different sizes and that even an American pint is smaller than a British pint. For these reasons the following information can do much to prevent many a spoilt cake:—

British measurements by the spoonful are taken as rounded spoonfuls
American measurements by the spoonful are always level

A British tablespoon = 4 teaspoons
An American tablespoon = 3 teaspoons
A British pint = 20 fluid oz
An American pint = 16 fluid oz

An American measuring cup = 8 fluid oz, and will hold approximately 4–4½ oz flour, 7 oz sugar and 7 oz butter or margarine. Incidentally flour should be sifted before being measured.

It is therefore useful if the kitchen measure has both scales marked, i. e., ¼, ½ and 1 pint marks and, in addition, liquid ounces.

GLOSSARY OF WORDS FREQUENTLY USED

Almonds	Nuts which are available to the home baker in the following forms:—whole, split, flaked, nibbed (i. e. chopped) and ground.
Almond paste	A stiff paste made from ground almonds, sugar and egg, used in icing cakes. It is also spoken of as marzipan.
Angelica	The stem of a plant preserved by candying in sugar. It is valued both on account of its green colour and pleasant flavour and is used as a decoration and in cakes.
Baking powder	Is an effervescing powder liberating carbon-dioxide when moistened. It is essentially made from bicarbonate of soda and cream of tartar and is generally purchased ready for use as a raising agent.
Baking soda	More correctly, bicarbonate of soda, effervesces if combined with an acid such as buttermilk, sour milk or cream of tartar and a liquid. It liberates carbon-dioxide and is used as a raising agent.

Bannock	A Scottish term denoting a flat, round cake.
Batter	A mixture made from flour with a liquid, generally eggs and milk. It is sometimes thick enough to drop from the point of a spoon.
Beating	Mixing with a quick rotary movement.
Biscuit	A dry, crisp cake. The literal translation from the Latin being twice cooked. This was originally necessary in order to dry them sufficiently to keep for a length of time. In America they use the word to denote a scone and refer to biscuits as cookies.
Blanch	To put into cold water and bring to boiling point. When baking, the object is generally to remove the skins from nuts.
Blend	To combine by stirring to a smooth consistency.
Bran	The inner husks of wheat or oats sifted away in the manufacture of flour.
Brush	To spread a thin coating of milk, egg, melted fat or other liquid over the top of food, e. g., scones.
Buttermilk	The milk that remains after the butter has been separated from the cream by churning. Sour milk may be used as a substitute for buttermilk.
Candied peel	Consists of the peel of the lemon, orange or citron, encrusted and preserved by sugar. It may be purchased in the form of whole caps or cut ready for use.
Caraway seeds	Aromatic seeds used as a flavouring.
Chocolate—bakers'	An easy-to-use chocolate for bakers not skilled in the handling of true chocolate. It melts readily to a liquid state.
Chocolate vermicelli	A cake decoration made from chocolate. It is also spoken of as chocolate hail-stones.
Choux	A light French pastry primarily used for éclairs and snowballs.
Combine	To mix ingredients.
Creaming	Mixing to a creamy softness.
Crème au beurre	A French form of butter icing, which includes either yolks or whites of egg in addition to the butter, sugar and flavouring.
Cutting in	Distributing a fat through a dry mixture by a cutting motion with a knife or pastry blender.
Dust	Sprinkling lightly with dry, powdery ingredients, such as flour or sugar.
Farls	A term, used in Irish and Scottish baking, referring to the traditional shape of bread. The circular cake is marked with a cross so

that it can be readily broken into quarters or farls after baking. Sometimes the cake may be cut into 6 or 8 wedges, as in making potato cake. These are still referred to as farls.

Fold in	To combine ingredients with a gentle down, up and over, movement of a spoon.
Friandises	"Dainties" or "dainty bits"—a name for very small decorative cakes prepared without baking.
Frosting	An American term for icing.
Golden syrup	A syrup obtained during the refining of sugar. It is lighter in colour and sweeter than treacle.
★*Griddle*	A round plate of cast-iron with a semi-circular handle. It is properly used over a turf fire. In Scotland the word 'girdle' is used instead of 'griddle' as in Ireland.
★*Harnen stand*	A traditional Irish cooking utensil used as a toaster or bread stand for harning or hardening bread after being baked on the griddle. It is generally of wrought iron and is often very ornamental.
Knead	To work dough with the knuckles or heel of the thumb, stretching it and then folding it over on itself.
Macaroon	A mixture made from almonds, sugar and the whites of eggs.
Marzipan or almond paste	A stiff paste made from ground almonds, sugar and egg. It is used for icing cakes.
Mille feuilles	Translated literally the term means "a thousand leaves". It refers to a cake made of several layers of puff pastry sandwiched with jam and cream.
Nut mill	A cooking utensil used for grinding nuts.
Oatmeal	The grain obtained from oats when dried and ground. There are three types—coarse or pin-head, medium and fine.
Parkin	A variety of gingerbread made with oatmeal.
Pitcaithley bannock (also spelt Pitcaithly)	A traditional Scottish recipe for a type of shortbread containing almonds, peel and, perhaps, caraways. It is sometimes decorated as well with caraways and peel.
Petits fours	A name which covers all kinds of very small decorative cakes. They are always baked as the name indicates, four meaning oven.
Potato bread or potato cake	A traditional Irish dish made from flour and boiled potatoes. It probably had its origin in difficult times. It is also spoken of as "fadge".

Potato ricer	A kitchen utensil used for pressing potatoes, to give a result similar to sieving.
Pot oven	A kind of Dutch oven used in traditional Irish kitchens. It may either be suspended over the turf fire or rest on a trivet. The lid is dished so that live turfs may be placed on top.
Rout biscuits	Very small decorative cakes made in England, in the past, to serve at fashionable evening parties or routs.
Rubbing in	Distributing a fat through a dry mixture, by rubbing with the thumb across the finger-tips, until the whole resembles fine bread-crumbs.
Scones	A variety of tea-cake originally cooked on a griddle but now more often baked in the oven.
"Soft Ball"	A term used when boiling a sugar syrup; it describes the condition at 240° F. To make the test, drop a little of the syrup into cold water, then try between the finger and thumb. If the temperature is 240° F it will form a soft ball.
Sugars	Granulated, castor (or caster) and icing (or confectioner's) sugar are all white sugars of increasing degrees of fineness. Demerara and soft brown sugar both have more flavour than the white sugars, not being so refined. Demerara sugar is coarse in the grain, while soft brown sugar is fine. Barbados sugar is a dark sugar of a similar colour to treacle. It is often used in fruit cakes to darken them.
"Thread"	A term used when boiling a sugar syrup; it describes the condition at 220° F—230° F. To make the test drop a little of the syrup into cold water, then try between the finger and thumb; it should form a thread. .
Treacle	A dark syrup obtained in refining sugar. It is not so sweet as golden syrup.
Whip	Beating eggs, cream, etc., with a brisk motion, to incorporate air into the mixture. Usually a whisk or rotary beater is used.
Wheaten meal	Meal made by grinding wheat. It is coarser and more flaky with the inner husk than wholemeal.
Wholemeal	A brown flour, ground from the whole wheat grain.
Yeast	A living organism used in aerating bread.

INDEX

Index

NOTES

NOTES